THE ART OF NOISE

DESTRUCTION OF MUSIC BY FUTURIST MACHINES

THE ART OF NOISE

DESTRUCTION OF MUSIC BY FUTURIST MACHINES

Russolo, Pratella, Marinetti, et al

ISBN 978-1-84068-686-9
Published 2023 by Deicide Press
First published by Sun Vision Press 2012

The Destruction Of Quadrature was translated by Anna Battista.
Futurism And Musical Notes by Daniele Lombardi first appeared in *Artforum* (translated by Meg Shore). Reprinted by permission.
Cover painting: "Mercurio che passa davanti al sole" by Giacomo Balla, 1914

CONTENTS

THE FUTURIST NOISE MACHINES

INTRODUCTION

FUTURISM AND MUSICAL NOTES

Discussions of Futurist music have been incorrect and misleading because after the period, musicians and critics have known only a concept of the music, which has been modified by subsequent theorizing and interpretation. Everything that does not fit into the theories has been regarded with suspicion, considered not to be music, and "relegated" to the domain of the visual arts or theater. History needs to be re-evaluated in terms of avant-garde movements such as Futurism so that those attempts that have opened the path to later artistic activity may be distinguishable from those which have fallen back on themselves, and have therefore failed to connect with the evolution of artistic thought.

Early in the 20th century the Italian musical world was characterized by the persistence of the late Romantic tradition, The curtain had already come down many times on Parsifal and on "program music", but the "season" continued (with inferior imitations). During this time one figure stands out as the initiator of a new musical concept (one that can be located at the root of Futurism and other avant-garde movements) – Ferruccio Busoni, who was also one of the greatest pianists of his time. Seeds of all the ideas that were later enthusiastically expressed by the Futurists Balilla Pratella and Luigi Russolo can be found in Busoni's essay, *Entwurf einer neuen Astetik der Tonkunst* ("Sketch For A New Aesthetic of Sound Art"), published in Trieste in 1907 by Schmidl.

Busoni speaks of "renewal" through a re-reading and

synthesizing of the past, In contrast to Filippo Tommaso Marinetti's "Let's destroy the museums and libraries," Busoni believed in the importance of tradition:

The transitory qualities of a work constitute the "modern", those qualities which are immutable preserve it from becoming "old fashioned". In the "modern" as in the "old" there is the good and the bad, the authentic and the false. In an absolute sense, the modern does not exist – in art there is only that which is born earlier and that which is born later – that which flowers for a long time and that which soon withers. There has always been the modern and there has always been the old.

This relationship to history is all that differentiates Busoni's programmatic principles from those of the Futurists. Coinciding with Busoni's concept of renewal, but more importantly revealing the relationship between Futurism and anti-traditionalism, Pratella begins his second manifesto with:

All innovators have, logically, been Futurists in relation to their times, Palestrina would have judged Bach mad, as Bach would have judged Beethoven, and as Beethoven would have judged Wagner.

The significance of Busoni's essay lies in his statement that traditional instruments were "tired". His intuitive recognition of new tonal possibilities allowed him to believe "...in abstract sound in technique without obstacles: in the limitlessness of sounds. Every effort, therefore, must lead toward a fresh source, a new beginning,."

Six years later Russolo applied himself to this process of innovation, writing: "We must break this restricted circle of pure sounds and conquer the infinite variety of noise-sounds." (This, also in order to come to terms with Beethoven and Wagner, but not through Busoni's solution of continuity.)

Microtonal research – which Busoni deals with amply (as do Charles Ives, Alois Hába and the later proponents of electronic sound) – is the basis for the application and practice of this new musical concept, which Russolo put into effect by constructing *intonarumori* or "noise-intoners". This decompositive process first explored by early Futurists, then adopted by the Dadaists, to finally become a characteristic of all the historical avant-gardes, is what really lies on the threshold between the 19th and 20th centuries. A sharp change had occurred in the definition of the nature of a musical work, now understood as a structure of sounds.

It is no accident that John Cage was one of the first musicians to be interested in Futurism and in Russolo's experiments. In 1946, when he had already created works for a prepared piano, he wrote:

In several of its important aspects, modern music of the twenties is known only by hearsay. The Italian "Art of Noise" established by Luigi Russolo has totally disappeared; in memory it is mistakenly associated with Marinetti. The work done with speech orchestras, divisions of the half-tone and electrical instruments is, for the most part, forgotten. Many composers exist today only as names.

Cage was absolutely correct; musicians like George Antheil are little-known, and the history of 20th-century music ought to be rewritten, giving a greater emphasis to the many artistic experiments of musicians who were neither appreciated nor encouraged during their lifetimes.

Contemporary music owes Busoni and the Futurists considerably more than has been acknowledged. They are responsible for fundamental innovations which were later developed in numerous ways throughout the 20th century:

1. Noise-sound, tone-research which led to the introduction of noise as a musical possibility.

2. Micro-spacing, research which has since been adopted by electronic music.

3. Improvisation, practiced since Russolo by most Futurist musicians and set out as a theory in a manitesto written in 1921 by Bartoccini and Vantia.

4. Simultaneity, an attempt at interweaving sound fragments – at the time this was an attitude parallel to, and contemporary with, that of Claude Debussy and Anton von Webern, although pointing in a contrary direction.

5. Interdisciplinary activity, a theatrical concept whereby the music flows and combines with mixed-media, taking forms other than traditional grand opera and ballet.

6. Mechanization, the myth of industrial society and of the machine, expressed by insistent isochronal rhythmic structures.

One of the first music critics in Italy to be interested in Futurist music was Luigi Pestalozza, who in a lengthy preface to the *Antologia della Rassegna Musicae* ("Anthology of Musical Reviews"), placed Pratella and Russolo in the broader context of Italian music.

Beyond any other consideration, the originality of the Futurists was in having caught the mechanistic and therefore technological spirit of the century – the rise of a super-industrialized mass society This had notable musical repercussions, although the Futurist contributions of Balilla Pratella and Luigi Russolo in this field were, above all, theoretical.

In an essay published in 1971 that discusses the relationship between Futurism and post-Second World War musicians, the composer Armando Gentilucci gives special attention to Pratella's *L'Aviatore Dro* ("Dro, the Aviator"), 1920, which he defines as "Future Expressionist". Although this long opera contains all the calls for spectacle of the early manifestoes (total action-theater of lights, colors, sounds, etc.), it still suffers from Pratella's provincialism and his idiosyncratic choices. His revolution was a storm in a teacup. (It is important to note that Pratella had studied under Mascagni.) Although *L'Aviatore Dro* did introduce aviation as a theme – one that continued on in such works as Luigo Dallapiccola's *Volo di Notte* ("Night Flight"), 1940 – it is really only an example of realism and popular entertainment.

Gentilucci asks: "Is there a relationship, a thread, which connects the post-war experimental avant-garde with Futurism?" He answers that one can assume a connection, citing Karlheinz Stockhausen, Cage and Luigi Nono as exponents of three different attitudes which he claims are all, in some way, related to the work of Pratella and Russolo. One could also answer his question by mentioning Fluxus or the many performances in the 60s and 70s, which were defined by the participants themselves as neo-Futurist. Pestalozza is absolutely right in saying: "Russolo's experiments avoided the problems of modern music and outshone them in every sense by proposing questions which were far too dangerous to handle." Russolo's background was that of a visual artist, rather than a professional musician. He was, therefore, quite far removed from the linguistic studies of the Conservatory composition classes, and was the first to have the courage to create something like noise-intoners – even if the kind of precedent as cited by Fred Prieberg in *Musica ex Machina* did already exist:

The close relationship between exotic music and noise was made public for the first time in the work of Carol-Bérard, who was born in 1885 and was a pupil of Isaac Albeniz. He not only studied and was influenced by primitive music and instruments, he also composed a ***Symphony of Mechanical Forces*** *in 1910, some years before Futurist interest in music. Moreover, he experimented with noises as music – he developed a notation system for noises,, and wrote on the problems of the instrumentation of noise music. It is not known however, whether he was a forerunner of, or if he formed later relationships with, the Futurists.*

Prieberg adds no further information. We know nothing more about Carol-Bérard, and the *Symphony of Mechanical Forces* has not been found.

Noise, according to this new definition, has two essential musical uses:

1. An onomatopoeic function as a signal which has precise connotations.

2. As a structural element in composition, and therefore a further tonal evolution in certain ways tied to late 19th century symphonism.

The first of these uses developed out of the Futurists *Poesia Sonora* ("Sound Poetry"), such as *Battaglia di Adrianopoli* ("Battle of Adrianople") by Mannetti, or *Onomatolingua* ("Onomata-Language") by Fortunato Depero. The second use was taken up by Russolo. In a manifesto of March 11, 1911 he says:

It will not be through a series of life-like noises but through the fantastic associations of these various tones and rhythms that the new orchestra will obtain the most complex and new sound emotions. Thus every instrument will have to be able to vary its tone and will have to extend its range to some degree.

In writing music of the city of the present and future, Russolo uses descriptive techniques which are somewhat similar to Debussy's realizations of pre-Raphaelite/Symbolist/ Impressionist compositions which evoke mood by "stopping" time; Russolo's noise of the city is different from Debussy's dreaminess, but it is nonetheless still a dream – the myth of the machine. Russolo's work has always been examined and judged by comparing the theories of the *Arte dei Rumori* ("Art of Noises") with the only existing document of noise-intoners, the 78 rpm recording, His Master's Voice R6919120, which contains two passages, *Corale* and *Serenata*. But these two compositions are by Antonio Russolo, Luigi Russolo's brother, a professional musician who used the noise-intoners together with other instruments. The record is misleading because the noise-intoners are used tamely, giving the impression of a commercial operation using his invention like at Bal Tabarin, which is harmful to Luigi's reputation. (The various scores that Luigi wrote have all been "lost or perhaps misplaced" by his brother Antonio, whose own work, on the other hand, has survived.)

I say this after having partially reconstructed seven bars of *Risveglio di una Citta* ("Awakening of a City") from the *Rete dei Rumori* ("Network of Noises") which Luigi Russolo published in 1914 in the magazine *Lacerba*. In 1977, when the Historic Archives of Contemporary Arts of the Venice Biennale organized an exhibition of Russolo's work, the curator, Gian

Franco Maffina, had five noise-intoners reconstructed for the occasion (Russolo's original instruments had all been destroyed during the Second World War). This permitted me to partially perform the fragment written by Russolo – "partially" because I was unable to use all nine types of noise-intoners indicated in his score. With a multi-track tape recorder I was able to realize only eight of the 12 "voices", and yet despite this, and in spite of living in the 1980s, after electronic music, the impact of the sound + emotion, which had previously been expressed only theoretically in the manifestoes, was impressive. (The comparison to Igor Stravinsky's *Le Sacre du Printemps*, published in 1913, is inevitable. While they are quite different in realization and expressiveness, these two pieces of music have analogous intentions. The noise-intoners must have had an incredible effect on the average listener of 1913, perhaps even stronger than that provoked by the *Sacre*.)

Just how can critics presume to judge these works without having ever heard even those 25 infernal seconds of *Risveglio di una Citta*, confusing the works of Antonio with those of Luigi? And ignoring the fact that Luigi's *Spirali di Rumori* ("Spirals of Noises"), was the first noise-intoners concert, probably introducing a practice of improvisation guided by outline? This practice, one of the fundamental tenets of Futurist aesthetics, is the form that comes closest to achieving the art of events in progress, of extemporaneous and unrepeatable gesture.

The 1921 manifesto of Bartoccini and Mantia represents the first theoretical enunciation of the idea of improvisation in music, and opened the way for this practice, which has become so widespread in the last 30 years. In a report to the 1924 Futurist Congress Franco Casavola stated:

As song and rhythm, music rises out of an improvised intoxication. Also in current music, the necessity of playing it imposes upon the performer a collaboration with the author in such a way that the performance envelops a necessary integration of the musical idea. The Futurist ideal is to identify the performer with the creator, to bring improvisation to everyone. The extemporaneous, ingenious element of music, conceived as being the real art of eloquence, frees music from traditional forms and modes.

These statements, together with those of Russolo, are probably the most important of the Futurist aesthetic. The three theoretical manifestoes by Pratella, which gave impetus to so much else, contain more passionate judgments than conceptual innovation (with the exception of the third manifesto, in which the discussions of rhythm touch upon an important theoretical aspect of music).

It is interesting to quote what Guido M. Gatti has said about Pratella's manifestoes:

The ***Distruzione Della Quadratura*** *("Destruction Of The Quadrature") of 1912, which is almost Pratella's war cry, emerges immediately after the more general manifestoes, and is directed, more than anything else, toward teaching and artistic conventions. Let us immediately say that everything in these pages can be accepted without fear of excommunication: in the year of our Lord nineteen-nineteen we have seen considerably more daring work in the musical avant-garde. So much so that Pratella's manifesto is not Futurism at all, but merely the recognition of a rhythmical freedom which every musician, from Wagner on, has achieved day by day, shedding his habits and his mental atavisms.*

Elsewhere in Europe, particularly in Paris and Vienna, other composers accomplished much more profound transformations of the compositional method. Pratella, however, retains the distinction of having started a new vision of the musical aesthetic in Italy with his first manifesto of 1910.

In Futurist music, the "implosion/explosion" evident in the paintings of Umberto Boccioni and Giacomo Balla was attempted, but the energizing of space and the sense of speed, the simultaneity and interaction. found no suitable equivalent in the music. Polyrhythmics sound like just another rhythmic composition, the result of the sum of the partial rhythms which constitute it; sound fragments, because of their linear nature, offer the listener "sequential" development, giving the impression of a series rather than the action of sounds. Silvio Mix's short *Profilo Sintetico Musicale di F.T. Marinetti* ("Synthetic Musical Profile of F. T. Marinetti"), 1924, is one example. The 36 bars are made up of 10 different parts. The execution of the passage does not give a clear sense of the interaction of fragments, but rather, the impression of an alogical, surreal juxtaposition. The *Profilo Sintetico Musicale* is an example of what must have been the kind of improvisations which Mix often did at Futurist soirées. Antonio Marasco, a Florentine Futurist painter and a friend of Mix's, referred to one of them:

I organized Futurist evenings at the Salone Materazzi in Via Martelli, and at Botto's in Via Cavour, or else I participated in those of the bookseller/publisher Ferrante Gonnelli who opened the first Permanent Futurist Gallery. During the exhibition Silvio Mix made extemporaneous interventions at the piano, improvising on themes dictated by the public. On some occasions there were three pianos and another friend of Mix's from Trieste would participate, along with Maestro Boghen, the Professor at the Conservatory, a strange sort of artist always under an enormous hat. When these "improvisations'" were held the public bought admission tickets which paid for everyone's dinner – a more lavish one for Professor Boghen, while Mix invariably ate rice and milk.

The system of musical collage and polyrhythm took a different form of realization with Darius Milhaud and George Antheil. The latter did not have direct relations with the Italian Futurists, although his *Jazz Symphony*, 1925, and *Ballet Méchanique* (the sound-track of Fernand Léger's film), are compositions which fit in perfectly with the Futurist aesthetic. The answer to this unsuccessful attempt to free musical timing is based on the belief in the myth of "isochrony" (contemporaneity), the symbol for the perfection of the new industrial world, which Prieberg called the "romanticism of the machine". The infuriating repetitiveness of the rhythm was meant to shock, to cause the "intoxication" described by Casavola, something that certainly occurs in Maurice Ravel's composition *Bolero*, 1928.

The most famous work deriving from the aesthetic of the machine is *Pacific 231*, 1923, by Arthur Honegger, an orchestral composition which describes in music the movements of a locomotive.

A brief but intense period of theatrical, ballet and pantomime activity opened with the advent of mechanistic music. The stage had been set for it by years of utopian literature and science fiction, and the new civilization of the machine appeared, mysterious, monstrous and transcendental by comparison with human, biological rhythms. Unfortunately, although we know of the existence of such works as the

Angoscia della Macchina ("Anguish of the Machine") by Silvio Mix to the text of Ruggero Vasari, which appears to have preceded Fritz Lang's famous film *Metropolis*, 1926, no examples of this activity have survived.

As in science fiction. futuristic worlds relate to the beginnings of the history of man. Images of archaic civilizations, prehistoric upheavals, suggest a journey through time, as do the innovations of the technological age. Along with the *Angoscia della Macchina* and *Astrale* by Mix, or the *Ballet Méchanique* by Antheil, there is *Le Sacre du Printemps* by Stravinsky, *Création* by Milhaud, and *Tides of Manaunaun* by Henry Dixon Cowell, another musician who was not in direct contact with the Futurists but who was very close to them.

The fact remains that the provincialism of Italian culture at that time, maintained by a middle class which supported Fascism, staunchly prevented the normal interchange of artistic information and experiences. This was manifested as a return to "traditionalism". Russolo strongly felt this involution, but saw no escape, and Casavola, after a lengthy interest in jazz, retreated in the face of censorship and actually destroyed all his own Futurist work.

The most important example of Italian mechanistic music is an orchestral page from *Cavalli + Acciaio* ("Horses + Steel"), "mechanicavalcade" for large orchestra, by Luigi Gral, a composer whom we otherwise know only by name (a piano transcription by the composer was published in 1935). This composition, like Ravel's *Bolero*, develops by means of a rhythmical structure, insistently repeats from start to finish and is made up of blocks of chords. The musical tempo indicated is *matto* (crazy).

Marinetti, the poet-animator of all Futurism, was the first to realize noise scores, preceding by many years Pierre

Schaeffer's *Concrete Music* and Cage's compositions, and anticipating the use of wireless sets. His *Cinque Sintesi per il Teatro Radiofonico* ("Five Syntheses for the Radiophonic Theater") is an application of the theories expressed in the *Radia* manifesto, and is composed of verbal scores which indicate the types and durations of sounds. Noises are assembled into a collage in which silence is an integral part. One of these syntheses includes a silence of three minutes – a completely new concept, a theater for radio, to be performed in a manner which suggests the existence of imagined space – this, 20 years before Cage's *4'33"*.

Futurist music did not have composers of the stature of Alban Berg, Schoenberg and Webern because, except for Pratella, no "professional" musician of any importance supported Marinetti s ideas, which were too advanced for the official musical climate of the day. As we know, Russolo was a painter, Mix a talented self-taught musician. Casavola, the professional, suffered a crisis and destroyed his Futurist scores in 1927. Virgilio Mortari was briefly a Futurist. as the improvisor in the *Teatro della Sorpresa* ("Theater of Surprise") and as the composer of the amusing *Foxtrot del Teatro della Sorpresa*. Although he is often classified as a Futurist (insofar as he was Modernist), Alfredo Casella, the musician who in some people's eyes could today be considered perhaps the most important figure of Italian music in the 20th century, in fact never adhered to the Futurist movement. Pratella states in his essay, *Musica Per Pianoforte Italiana*, March 19. 1916:

If even on the surface Casella's music seems harmonically and aesthetically more daring than Futurist music, one must nevertheless not mistake it for Futurist music, since it is substantially removed from this, as indeed it is from the music of the French or Russian avant-garde.

Casella's work is still within the realm of impressionism, and the exceptional effort of sensitivity. The music in flux starts out from an intimate musical state of mind, stimulator of a lyrical deformation and a purely musical and not programmatic and coloristic construction. By this I do not mean to lessen the intrinsic worth of Casella s music, I mean only to define and to distinguish it.

Casella lived in Paris during the years 1910-15, and there breathed a freer cultural climate than that of Italy. His *Trois Pièces pour Pianola*, 1917, is one of the most important expressions which, in large part, derive from Futurist theories.

Russolo and the other Futurists, with the advent of Fascism, were restricted, not so much by Marinetti's artistic choices, but because the regime, from 1922 on, favored a policy of historic self-justification and put the mechanics of tradition into motion, attempting officially to tie musical experimentation to the schools and to categorize precisely defined styles which concentrated on reviving academicism. The *Corpol delle Nuove Musiche* ("Corporation of New Music") was founded in Rome in 1923, with Gabriele D Annunzio, G. Francesco Malipiero and Alfredo Casella as its directors and Bernardino Molinari and Ildebrando Pizzetti as advisors. The numerous aims of the corporation were the complete antithesis of Futurist theories. In the course of time Fascism supported precisely those musicians like Alfano, Casella, Malipiero, Pizzetti and Respighi, who forged a compromise between past and future with works and themes which lay within the linguistic and semantic boundaries that the Fascist regime did not deem dangerous. These musicians were responsible for the systematic elimination of all traces of Futurism, and Russolo's noise-intoners paid the price. The musical spectacles with which the Futurists experimented were totally replaced by sweet little operas and cumbersome grand operas that tried to align themselves with the kind of "sacred values" that were slowly reduced to a mockery in travertine architecture.

Russolo's decompositive attitude was an easy target for charges of dilettantism, while Respighi's *Fountains of Rome* and *Pines of Rome*, although works of unquestionable value, could be used by the Fascists as evidence of "quality' and of the value of the "new Italian musical style" which these musicians championed.

In *La Prora* ("The Prow"), Casella ends his essay with:

Besides, the future will sooner or later have its say, and it will know how to brilliantly set apart the few real "creators" of today – for whom the new sound technicalities are nothing more than simple means which are indispensable for reaching unknown forms of beauty – from the innumerable false revolutionaries, who use these same means in a clumsy and naive way with the sole aim of achieving immediate and ephemeral celebrity.

The reference to the Futurists is clear enough, even though Casella's tactic, followed by most of the others, was systematically to ignore all artistic activities which stemmed from Futurism.

As early as 1911, Pratella's manifestoes had been checked to the extent that Pizzetti wrote to Malipiero:

Regarding what you wrote me concerning the necessity of having faith in a better future for the fortunes of us young Italian musicians, and concerning the need to unite in a compact group, acting for the common interest, I am somewhat skeptical. As regards myself, I am and shall always be ready to give of myself, with my own energy and with my own work, to do everything of which I am capable, but who else will know how to do the same? Will you be there? All right, I believe you. Will Bastiani be there? Very well, we shall be three. And then? Just think my friend, against us there are already musicians like Zandonai and Pratella – that is, sly profiteers and crafty ignoramuses – dozens of them! And we – or I at least – we are naive compared to them!

In essence, Futurism grew so weak that it disappeared with the advent of Fascism, which favoured the kinds of artistic expression that would consolidate its power. It is also true that among the Futurist musicians there was no one figure who managed to establish himself or the aesthetics of Futurist music by producing anything of truly great significance. As the poet Francesco Cangiullo wrote in his autobiography:

...apropos the musicians Casavola and I (whose names have only been touched upon in this book but can be found in the last Futurist lists) and the painters Depero, and Prampolini, that Casavola and Mortari musicians of unquestionable value, in reality never did know how to compose what might have been Futurist music, nor did Baililla Pratella. The unsurpassed innovative composer of that period was Stravinsky.

THE ART OF NOISE

DESTRUCTION OF MUSIC BY FUTURIST MACHINES

PRATELLA, RUSSOLO

MANIFESTO OF FUTURIST MUSICIANS

FRANCESCO BALILLA PRATELLA

11 October 1910

I appeal to the young. Only they should listen, and only they can understand what I have to say. Some people are born old, slobbering spectres of the past, cryptograms swollen with poison. To them no words or ideas, but a single injunction: the end.

I appeal to the young, to those who are thirsty for the new, the actual, the lively. They follow me, faithful and fearless, along the roads of the future, gloriously preceded by my, by our, intrepid brothers, the Futurist poets and painters, beautiful with violence, daring with rebellion, and luminous with the animation of genius.

A year has passed since a jury composed of Pietro Mascagni, Giacomo Orefice, Guglielmo Mattioli, Rodolfo Ferrari and the critic Gian Battista Nappi announced that my musical Futurist work entitled La Sina d'Vargöun, based on a free verse poem, also by me, had won a prize of 10,000 lire against all other contenders. This prize was to cover the cost of performance of the work thus recognized as superior and worthy, according to the bequest of the Bolognese, Cincinnato Baruzzi.

The performance, which took place in December 1909, in the Teatro Comunale in Bologna, brought with it success in the form of enthusiasm, base and stupid criticisms, generous defense on the part of friends and strangers, respect and imitation from my enemies.

After such a triumphal entry into Italian musical society and after establishing contact with the public, publishers and critics, I was able to judge with supreme serenity the intellectual mediocrity, commercial baseness and misoneism that reduce Italian music to a unique and almost unvarying form of vulgar melodrama, an absolute result of which is our inferiority when compared to the Futurist evolution of music in other countries.

In Germany, after the glorious and revolutionary era dominated by the sublime genius of Wagner, Richard Strauss almost elevated the baroque style of instrumentation into an essential form of art, and although he cannot hide the aridity, commercialism and banality of his spirit with harmonic affectations and skillful, complicated and ostentatious acoustics, he nevertheless does struggle to combat and overcome the past with innovatory talent.

In France, Claude Debussy, a profoundly subjective artist and more a literary man than a musician, swims in a diaphanous and calm lake of tenuous, delicate, clear blue and constantly transparent harmonies. He presents instrumental symbolism and a monotonous polyphony of harmonic sensations conveyed through a scale of whole tones-a new system, but a system nevertheless, and consequently a voluntary limitation. But even with these devices he is not always able to mask the scanty value of his one-sided themes and rhythms and his almost total lack of ideological development. This development consists, as far as he is concerned, in the primitive and infantile periodic repetition of a short and poor theme, or in rhythmic, monotonous and vague progressions. Having returned in his operatic formulae to the stale concepts of Florentine chamber music which gave birth to melodrama in the seventeenth century, he has still not yet succeeded in completely reforming the music drama of his country. Nevertheless, he more than any other fights the past valiantly and there are many points at which he overcomes it. Stronger than Debussy in ideas, but musically inferior, is G. Charpentier.

In England, Edward Elgar is cooperating with our efforts to destroy the past by pitting his will to amplify classical symphonic forms, seeking richer ways of thematic development and multiform variations on a single theme. Moreover, he directs his energy not merely to the exuberant variety of the instruments, but to the variety of their combinational effects, which is in keeping with our complex sensibility.

In Russia, Modeste Mussorgsky, renewed by the spirit of Nikolai Rimsky-Korsakov, grafts the primitive national element on to the formulae inherited from others, and by seeking dramatic truth and harmonic liberty he abandons tradition and consigns it to oblivion. Alexander Glazunov is moving in the same direction, although still primitive and far from a pure and balanced concept of art.

In Finland and Sweden, also, innovatory tendencies are being nourished by means of national musical and poetical elements, and the works of Sibelius confirm this.

And in Italy?

The vegetating schools, conservatories and academies act as snares for youth and art alike. In these hot-beds of impotence, masters and professors, illustrious deficients, perpetuate traditionalism and combat any effort to widen the musical field.

The result is prudent repression and restriction of any free and daring tendency; constant mortification of impetuous intelligence; unconditioned propping-up of imitative and incestuous mediocrity; prostitution of the great glories of the music of the past, used as insidious arms of offense against budding talent; limitation of study to a useless form of acrobatics floundering in the perpetual last throes of a behindhand culture that is already dead.

The young musical talents stagnating in the conservatories have their eyes fixed on the fascinating mirage of opera under the protection of the big publishing houses. Most of them end up bad-and all the worse for lack of ideological and technical foundations. Very few get so far as to see their work staged, and most of these pay out money to secure venal and ephemeral successes, or polite toleration.

Pure symphony, the last refuge, harbors the failed opera composers, who justify themselves by preaching the death of the music drama as an absurd and anti-musical form. On the other hand they confirm the traditional claim that the Italians are not born equipped for the symphony, revealing themselves equally inept in this most noble and vital form of composition. The cause of their double failure is unique, and is not to be sought in the completely guiltless and incessantly slandered forms of opera and symphony, but in the writers' own impotence.

They make use, in their ascent to fame, of that absurd swindle that is called well-made music, the falsification of all that is true and great, a worthless copy sold to a public that lets itself be cheated by its own free will.

But the rare fortunates who, through multiple renunciations, have managed to obtain the protection of the large publishers, to whom they are tied by illusory and humiliating noose-contracts, these represent the classes of serfs, cowards and those who voluntarily sell themselves.

The great publisher-merchants rule over everything; they impose commercial limitations on operatic forms, proclaiming which models are not to be excelled, unsurpassable: the base, rickety and vulgar operas of Giacomo Puccini and Umberto Giordano.

Publishers pay poets to waste their time and intelligence in concocting and seasoning-in accordance with the recipes of that grotesque pastry cook called Luigi Illica-that fetid cake that goes by the name of opera libretto.

Publishers discard any opera that surpasses mediocrity, since they have a monopoly to disseminate and exploit their wares and defend the field of action from any dreaded attempt at rebellion.

Publishers assume protection and power over public taste, and, with the complicity of the critics, they evoke as example or warning amidst the tears and general chaos, our alleged Italian monopoly of melody and of bel canto, and our never sufficiently praised opera, that heavy and suffocating crop of our nation.

Only Pietro Mascagni, the publishers' favourite, has had the spirit and power to rebel against the traditions of art, against publishers and the deceived and spoilt public. His personal example, first and unique in Italy, has unmasked the infamy of publishing monopolies and the venality of the critics. He has hastened the hour of our liberation from commercial czarism and dilettantism in music; Pietro Mascagni has shown great talent in his real attempts at innovation in the harmonic and lyrical aspects of opera, even though he has not yet succeeded in freeing himself from traditional forms.

The shame and filth that I have denounced in general terms faithfully represent Italy's past in its relationship with art and with the customs of today: industry of the dead, cult of cemeteries, parching of the vital sources.

Futurism, the rebellion of the life of intuition and feeling, quivering and impetuous spring, declares inexorable war on doctrines, individuals and works that repeat, prolong or exalt the past at the expense of the future. It proclaims the conquest of amoral liberty, of action, conscience and imagination. It proclaims that Art is disinterest, heroism and contempt for easy success.

I unfurl to the freedom of air and sun the red flag of Futurism, calling to its flaming symbol such young composers as have hearts to love and fight, minds to conceive, and brows free of cowardice. And I shout with joy at feeling myself unfettered from all the chains of tradition, doubt, opportunism and vanity.

I, who repudiate the title of Maestro as a stigma of mediocrity and ignorance, hereby confirm my enthusiastic adhesion to Futurism, offering to the young, the bold and the reckless these my irrevocable conclusions:

1. To convince young composers to desert schools, conservatories and musical academies, and to consider free study as the only means of regeneration.

2. To combat the venal and ignorant critics with assiduous contempt, liberating the public from the pernicious effects of their writings, and to found with this aim in view a musical review that will be independent and resolutely opposed to the criteria of conservatory professors and to those of the debased public.

3. To abstain from participating in any competition with the customary closed envelopes and related admission charges, denouncing all mystifications publicly, and unmasking the incompetence of juries, which are generally composed of fools and impotents.

4. To keep at a distance from commercial or academic circles, despising them, and preferring a modest life to bountiful earnings acquired by selling art.

5. The liberation of individual musical sensibility from all imitation or influence of the past, feeling and singing with the spirit open to the future, drawing inspiration and aesthetics from nature, through all the human and extra-human phenomena present in it. Exalting the man-symbol everlastingly renewed by the varied aspects of modern life and its infinity of intimate relationships with nature.

6. To destroy the prejudice for "well-made" music-rhetoric and impotence-to proclaim the unique concept of Futurist music, as absolutely different from music to date, and so to shape in Italy a Futurist musical taste, destroying doctrinaire, academic and soporific values, declaring the phrase "let us return to the old masters" to be hateful, stupid and vile.

7. To proclaim that the reign of the singer must end, and that the importance of the singer in relation to a work of art is the equivalent of the importance of an instrument in the orchestra.

8. To transform the title and value of the "operatic libretto" into the title and value of "dramatic or tragic poem for music", substituting free verse for metric structure. Every opera writer must absolutely and necessarily be the author of his own poem.

9. To combat categorically all historical reconstructions and traditional stage sets and to declare the stupidity of the contempt felt for contemporary dress.

10. To combat the type of ballad written by Tosti and Costa, nauseating Neapolitan songs and sacred music which, having no longer any reason to exist, given the breakdown of faith, has become the exclusive monopoly of impotent conservatory directors and a few incomplete priests.

11. To provoke in the public an ever-growing hostility towards the exhumation of old works which prevents the appearance of innovators, to encourage the support and exaltation of everything in music that appears original and revolutionary, and to consider as an honor the insults and ironies of moribunds and opportunists.

And now the reactions of the traditionalists are poured on my head in all their fury. I laugh serenely and care not a jot; I have climbed beyond the past, and I loudly summon young musicians to the flag of Futurism which, launched by the poet Marinetti in *Le Figaro* in Paris, has in a short space of time conquered most of the intellectual centres of the world.

TECHNICAL MANIFESTO OF FUTURIST MUSIC

FRANCESCO BALILLA PRATELLA

11 March 1911

All innovators have logically been Futurists in relation to their time. Palestrina would have judged Bach crazy, and thus Bach would have judged Beethoven, and thus Beethoven would have judged Wagner. Rossini boasted of having finally understood the music of Wagner by reading it in reverse! Verdi, after an audition of the overture of Tannhauser, called Wagner insane in a letter to one of his friends!

We are, therefore, at the window of a glorious mental hospital, while we declare, without hesitation, that counterpoint and the fugue, still considered today as the most important branch of musical education, do not represent anything other than the ruins belonging to the history of polyphony, properly of that period that runs from the Flemish until J. S. Bach.

In their place, harmonic polyphony, the rational fusion of counterpoint and harmony, will prevent the musician, once and for all, from splitting himself between two cultures: a trespasser on some other century, as well as part of his own contemporary culture; these being irreconcilable with each other because the products of the two are very different in manner of feeling and conception. The second, for logical reasons of progress and evolution, is already a remote and unattainable consequence of the first by having summarised, transformed, and surpassed it by a great distance.

Harmony, historically a matter of course in the melody-played subsequently according to diverse modes of the scale-was born when each sound of the melody was considered in relationship to the combinations of all the other sounds in the mode of the scale to which it belonged.

In such a manner, there developed an understanding that the melody is an expressive synthesis of a harmonic succession. Today people cry and lament that the young musicians no longer know how to find melody, alluding, no doubt, to those of Rossini, Bellini, Verdi, and Ponchielli.... Instead, these musicians conceive of the melody harmonically; they hear harmony through different and more complex combinations and successions of sounds and then find new foundations for melodies.

Young musicians, once and for all, will stop being vile imitators of the past that no longer has a reason for existing and imitators of the venal flatterers of the public's base taste.

We Futurists proclaim that the diverse modes of old scales, the various sensations of major, minor, augmented, diminished, and also the very recent modes of scales for internal tones are none other than simple details of a unique harmonic and atonal mode of a chromatic scale. We declare, moreover, that the values of consonance and dissonance are non-existent.

The Futurist melody will be embellished by the innumerable combinations and by the various relationships that derive from them. This other melody will only be the synthesis of harmony, similar to thousands of sea waves in unequal crests.

We Futurists proclaim as progress and as a victory of the future the chromatic atonal mode, the research and realisation of the enharmonic mode. Whereas chromatism uniquely rewards us with all the sounds contained in a scale that is divided into minor and major semitones, enharmonic music, by using even smaller subdivisions of tones, will offer in addition the maximum number of interminable and combined sounds to our renewed sensibility. Enharmonic music will also permit the newest and most varied relations of chords and timbres.

But above all, enharmonic music renders the possibility of intonation and the natural and instinctive modulations of enharmonic intervals, which at present are not feasible, given the artificiality of our scale within the tempered system that we wish to overcome. For a long time we Futurists have loved these enharmonic intervals that we find only in the dissonance of an orchestra when the instruments play out of tune and in the spontaneous songs of the people when they are intoned without a knowledge of art.

The rhythm of dance: monotonous, limited, decrepit, and barbarous, will have to yield its rule of polyphony to a free polyrhythmic process and limit itself to remaining a characteristic detail of it. Therefore, one must recognise that a relationship between even, uneven, and mixed tempos is possible just as the relationship between binary, ternary, ternary-binary, and binary-ternary rhythms is accepted. For example, one or more bars of uneven tempo placed in the middle or at the end of a musical phrase, which is either in even or mixed tempo or vice versa, cannot be considered wrong by using the ridiculous rules and fallacies of the so-called quadratura [continuous steady rhythm], the disgraceful umbrella of all the impotents who teach in the conservatories.

The technical knowledge of instrumentation must be conquered experimentally. The instrumental composition may be conceived by imagining and hearing a particular orchestra for every particular and diverse musical condition of inspiration.

All this will be possible when the conservatories, schools, and academies are deserted and closed and when the necessity of experience is finally provided for by giving a character of absolute freedom to musical studies. The masters of today, transformed into the experts of tomorrow, will be the guides and objective collaborators of the studious. They will cease from their unconscious corruption of budding geniuses that they have caused by suppressing them with their own personalities and by imposing their own errors and criteria on them.

For man the absolute truth is in what he feels as a human being. The artist, by purely interpreting nature, makes nature human.

Sky, water, forests, rivers, mountains, the entanglements of ships, and swarming cities are transformed through the soul of the musician into marvellous and powerful voices that humanly sing the passions and the desires of man, his joy and his sorrows, and they are revealed to him by virtue of art as the common and indissoluble bond that binds him to all the rest of nature.

The musical forms are none other than an aspect and a fragment of a unique and complete whole. Every form exists in relation to the potentiality of expression, to the development of a passionate and generated motive, and to the sensibility and intuition of the artistic creator. Rhetoric and pompousness, proceeding from a disproportion between the passionate motive and its explanatory form, produce, for the most part, cases influenced and blinded by traditions, culture, environment, and often by cerebral limitations.

The only passionate motive imposed on the musician is

his own formal and synthetic explanation, since synthesis is the cardinal property of expression of musical aesthetics.

The contrast of several passionate motives and the relationship between their potential of expansion and development constitute symphony.

The Futurist symphony considers as its maximum forms: the symphonic, orchestral, and vocal poem, and the theatrical opera.

The pure symphonist, drawing from his passionate motives, developments, contrasts, lines, and forms, with ample and free imagination, must not conform to any criterion that is not a result of his artistic sense of equilibrium and proportion, but he must find his goal in the complex of expressive means and proper aesthetics of pure musical art. This sense of Futurist equilibrium is nothing more than the attainment of maximum intensity of expression.

The opera composer, in contrast, attracts all the reflections of other arts into his orbit of inspiration and musical aesthetics-in powerful competition with the multiplication of expressive and communicative effectiveness. The opera composer must conceive these other secondary elements as being controlled by his inspiration and musical aesthetics.

The human voice, also being a maximum means of expression because it is ours and comes from us, will be surrounded by the orchestra, sonorous atmosphere full of all the voices of nature, rendered through art.

The vision of a poem written as a scenario leaps to the imagination of the artistic creator to meet his particular necessity, emerging from a wish to explain the generated and inspired passionate motives. The dramatic or tragic poem will not be able to be conceived with the music if it is not the result of a musical state of inspiration and a unique vision of musical aesthetics. The opera composer, creating rhythms in connection with the words, already creates musically and is the only author of his own opera. By writing music for the poetry of others, instead, he stupidly renounces his particular fountain of original inspiration, his musical aesthetics, and takes the rhythmic part of his melody from others.

Free verse is the only suitable one, not being bound by the limitations of rhythm and of accents monotonously repeated in restricted and insufficient formulas. The polyphonic wave of human poetry finds every rhythm, every accent, and every mode in free verse. These are necessary for the exuberant expression of itself as in a charming symphony of words. Such freedom of rhythmic expression is certainly Futurist music.

Man and the multitudes of men on the stage must no longer imitate common speech phonically but must sing, as when we, unconscious of the place and the work, seized by a deep wish to expand and to dominate, burst out instinctively in essential and charming human language: natural, spontaneous song, without the music of rhythm or of intervals, artificial limitations of expressions that sometimes make us regret the efficiency of words.

We conclude:

It is necessary to conceive of melody as a "synthesis of harmony," considering the harmonic definitions of major, minor, augmented, and diminished as simple details of a unique chromatic atonal mode.

Consider enharmonic music as a magnificent conquest by Futurism.

Crush the domination of dance rhythm, considering this

rhythm as a detail of free rhythm, just as the hendecasyllable can be a detail of the strophe in free verse.

Create polyphony in an absolute sense by fusing harmony and counterpoint; never tried until today.

Take possession of all the expressive, technical, and dynamic values of the orchestra, and consider instrumentation as an aspect of universal sound that is incessantly mobile and that constitutes a unique whole through the fusion of all its parts.

Consider musical form consistent and dependent on generated passionate motives.

Do not mistake the usual traditional dead and buried schemes of symphony for symphonic form.

Conceive of theatrical opera as a symphonic form.

Proclaim that the musician must be the author of dramatic or tragic poems for his music. The symbolic action of the poem must leap to the imagination of the musician, urged by his wish to explain passionate motives. The written verses of others require the musician to accept the rhythm for his own music from others.

Recognise free verse as the only way to arrive at a criterion of polyrhythmic freedom.

Contain in music all the new attitudes of nature that are

always tamed by man in different ways by virtue of his incessant scientific discoveries. Give musical animation to crowds, great industrial shipyards, trains, transatlantic steamers, battleships, automobiles, and aeroplanes. Add the domination of the machine and the victorious reign of Electricity to the great central motive of a musical poem.

THE DESTRUCTION OF QUADRATURE

FRANCESCO BALILLA PRATELLA

18 July 1912

THE RHYTHM is a pulsating human heart; its PAUSES and MOVEMENTS are waves of living blood that flood in and SPILL OUT.
THE HAND MOVEMENT, conceived as a time measuring unit in the same way as the foot that beats on the ground in a dance routine, is the BACKBONE OF THE RHYTHM.
MOVEMENT OF TWO TONES (a PAUSE and a MOVEMENT) = BINARY RHYTHM
MOVEMENT OF THREE TONES (a pause and two MOVEMENTS) = TRINARY RHYTHM.
THE TONES are consequently BINARILY AND TRINARILY DIVIDED into SUBTONES made of PAUSES and MOVEMENTS, in the same fashion of tones, but in a proportion minor of a half and a third.
The different ways the BINARY AND TRINARY RHYTHMS are alternated together produces the MIXED RHYTHM.
THE BINARY RHYTHM MOVEMENT offers TWO COMBINATIONS OF MIXED SUBDIVISIONS: *a* = (BIN-TER), *b* = (TER-BIN).
THE TRINARY RHYTHM MOVEMENT offers SIX COMBINATIONS of a MIXED SUBDIVISION: *a* = (BIN-BIN-TER.), *b* = (TER-BIN-BIN.), *c* = (BIN-TER-TER.), *d* = (TER-TER-BIN.), *e* = (BIN-TER-BIN.), *f* = (TER-BIN-TER.).

To recap:

BINARY RHYTHM		BINARY SUBDIVISION TRINARY SUBDIVISION
	MOVEMENT	MIXED (N. 2 COMBINATIONS) SUBDIVISION
TRINARY RHYTHM		BINARY SUBDIVISION TRINARY SUBDIVISION MIXED (N. 6 COMBINATIONS)

The relations highlighted between TONE and MOVEMENT are the same existing between MOVEMENT and TIME SIGNATURE.
TIME SIGNATURE of 2 MOVEMENTS or of a number of movements MULTIPLE of 2 (ONE PAUSE and TWO MOVEMENTS and so on) = BINARY MEASURE.
TIME SIGNATURE of 3 MOVEMENTS or of a number of movements MULTIPLE OF 2 (ONE PAUSE and TWO MOVEMENTS and so on) = TRINARY MEASURE; independently from every single kind of rhythm relating to each movement.
The different way in which the MOVEMENTS OF BINARY RHYTHM are matched with the MOVEMENTS OF TRINARY RHYTHM and viceversa during A TIME SIGNATURE produces as succession of MOVEMENTS OF MIXED RHYTHM.
The union of a BINARY TIME SIGNATURE with a TRINARY TIME SIGNATURE and viceversa, produces a MIXED TIME SIGNATURE:

To recap:

			BINARY SUB.
			TRINARY SUB.
T	BINARY WITH MOVEMENTS OF	BINARY RHYTHM OF	MIXED SUB.
I			
			BINARY SUB.
			TRINARY SUB.
		TRINARY RHYTHM OF	MIXED SUB.
M			
E		MIXED RHYTHM OF	BINARY SUB.
			TRINARY SUB.
			MIXED SUB.
			BINARY SUB.
			TRINARY SUB.
S	TRINARY WITH MOVEMENTS OF	BINARY RHYTHM OF	MIXED SUB.
I			BINARY SUB.
			TRINARY SUB
		TRINARY RHYTHM OF	MIXED SUB.
G			
N		MIXED RHYTHM OF	BINARY SUB.
			TRINARY SUB
			MIXED SUB.
A			
T			BINARY SUB.
			TRINARY SUB
U	MIXED WITH MOVEMENTS OF	BINARY RHYTHM OF	MIXED SUB.
R			BINARY SUB.
			TRINARY SUB
		TRINARY RHYTHM OF	MIXED SUB.
E			
		MIXED RHYTHM OF	BINARY SUB.
			TRINARY SUB
			MIXED SUB.

Therefore:

1. THE COMMON CONCEPTS OF ODD AND EVEN TIME SIGNATURES ARE WRONG.

The time signatures 3/4 and 9/8 are found classified among the ODD TIME SIGNATURES. The time signatures 5/4 and 7/4 – in a MIXED TIME SIGNATURE – should therefore belong to the CLASS OF ODD TIME SIGNATURES as well, since 5 and 7 are ODD numbers like 3 and 9. So?

The time signature 6/8 classified among the EVEN TIME SIGNATURES, since multiples of 2 belong to the BINARY TIME SIGNATURE in the same way as 3 belongs to the TRINARY TIME SIGNATURE.

The old classification between EVEN AND ODD TIMES is therefore INCORRECT, MISINTERPRETING and CONFUSING the CONCEPT OF TIME.

THEREFORE TIME SIGNATURES will have to be divided in the following way:

BINARY MEASURE TIME SIGNATURES = THE MOVEMENT MULTIPLIED BY 2 OR BY ITS MULTIPLES.

TRINARY MEASURE TIME SIGNATURES = THE MOVEMENT MULTIPLIED BY 3 OR BY ITS MULTIPLES.

MIXED MEASURE TIME SIGNATURES = A COMBINATION OF TWO PREVIOUS GENRES (BIN-TER) AND (TER-BIN).

The synthesis of this PRINCIPLE – a natural law definying the rhythm of music – is completed in the following way:

BINARY RHYTHM TONE AND SUBTONE = THE MOVEMENT DIVIDED BY 2 AND BY ITS MULTIPLES.

TRINARY RHYTHM TONE AND SUBTONE = THE MOVEMENT DIVIDED BY 3 AND BY ITS MULTIPLES.

The formation of a MIXED RHYTHM was already sufficiently explained.

2. THE BINARY RHYTHM AND THE TRINARY RHYTHM ARE SYNCHRONOUS AND EQUIVALENT.

TWO SUBTONES, TWO TONES and TWO MOVEMENTS

ARE EQUIVALENT to THREE SUBTONES, THREE TONES and THREE MOVEMENTS and viceversa, for the same duration of time. For this reason TWO TIME SIGNATURES featuring the same number of movements belonging to different types of rhythms, are said to be CONNECTED among them.
Such time signatures are therefore also SYNCHRONOUS and EQUIVALENT. THE MOVEMEMENT STOPS WITH A PAUSE, THE TIME SIGNATURE STARTS WITH A MOVEMENT AND WITH A PAUSE. BINARY AND TRINARY TIME MEASURES are therefore achieved via TONES AND MOVEMENTS; the latter depends anyway from the IDENTIC AND UNIQUE INITIAL TONE AND PAUSE for the two types of rhythm.
A new common mistake is destroyed by this law: that of conceiving the THIRD TONE in the TRINARY RHYTHM and the third movement in the TRINARY TIME SIGNATURE as a PAUSE for two reasons:
BECAUSE THE IMMEDIATE SUCCESSION OF TWO TONES OR PAUSES IS NOT POSSIBLE.
BECAUSE TWO RHYTHMS, ONE WITH A PAUSE AND A MOVEMENT, THE OTHER WITH A PAUSE, A MOVEMENT AND ANOTHER PAUSE, CAN NOT BE CONSIDERED AS SYNCHRONOUS AND EQUIVALENT.
3. THE MAXIMUM RHYTHMIC EFFICACY MANIFESTS ITSELF THROUGH THE MELODIC EXPRESSION; THE POLYPHONIC COMPLICATION NEUTRALISES THE RHYTHMIC EFFICACY.
The present axiom, focus of all futuristic music, will later on find new and definite conclusions pertaining to it.
For the time being I would like to focus on the fact that since musical expression is a synthesis – A MELODIC THOUGHT – the numerous elements that take part in it must partially and

proportionally sacrifice their individuality and cooperate together towards the exaltation of the SYNTHETIC effect.

Beethoven and Rossini knew this principle very well; for this reason their music sounds more varied rhythm-wise than Wagner or Strauss', though in their case rhythm assumed a variety of movements that was never reached not even in a dream by the two other maestros.

Strauss drowned rhythm in rhythm, juxtaposing rhythms to other rhythms and neutralising one with the other, generating ARRHYTHMICS.

In practice the JUXTAPOSITION OF TWO DIFFERENT RHYTHMS is effective until it can be REGULATED WITH THE MOVEMENTS; when this doesn't happen it produced ARRHYTHMIC CONFUSION and SIMULTANEOUS, PRECISE AND EXACT EXECUTION of one type of rhythms becomes almost impossible.

As an example we can use the first bars of the prelude of Wagner's *Parsifal*: the juxtaposition of a TRINARY RHYTHM ENTRUSTED TO THE AEROPHONES (6/4 = 3 + 3) in a BINARY RHYTHM ENTRUSTED TO THE CHORDOPHONES (4/4 = 2 + 2 SLOW. The simultaneous execution of the two rhythms will never result CLEAR and PRECISE, since ONE BATON BEATING TWO MOVEMENTS is not a good guide to CALCULATE THREE MOVEMENTS.

4. AFTER THE ABOVE-MENTIONED CONCLUSIONS, IT IS ABSOLUTELY NECESSARY TO FIND A NEW WAY TO KEEP THE TIME CORRESPONDING IN A CORRECT AND EXACT WAY TO THE CONCEPT OF TIME.

The present marks do not take into consideration TIME RELATIVITY, they do not express the different CONFORMATION OF THE MIXED TIME SIGNATURES and conceptually alter the RELATIVITY OF THE VALUES OF

MUSICAL FIGURES.
Even Strauss in FORMALLY CONCEIVING his music, made mistakes of RHYTHMIC RELATIVITY.
I'm taking as examples extracts from the *Salomé* (French-Italian reduction for voice and piano).
Page 30. NARRABOTH: *Divina, non lo posso, nol posso...* (My divine, I can't, I can't....)
(TIME CUT against 3/4) – MISTAKE OF RELATIVITY.
Page 20. SECOND SOLDIER: *...questo noi non lo sappiam, augusta* (we don't know this, oh divine)
(4/4 against ?) – UNEXCUSABLE MISTAKE!

A new system of taking time into consideration and marking it

BINARY RHYTHM MOVEMENT: 12 = (2/8 - 1/4) RELATED TO MOVEMENT OF TRINARY RHYTHM :

13 = (3/8 - 3/4)

Binary time signature :
22 = (2/2 - CUT TIME) related to 23 = (6/8 - 6/4);

42 = (ORDINARY TIME – 4/4)

related to 43 = (12/8 - 12/4);

4 + 22 = (.........) related to = 4 + 23 = (.........);

Trinary time signature:
32 = (3/4 – 3/2) related to 33 = (9/8 – 9/4);

3 + 32 = (6/8 – 6/4) related to 3 + 33 = (.........).

Mixed time signature:
2 + 32 = (5/4) related to 2 + 33 = (.........);

3 + 22 = (5/4) related to 3 + 23 = (.........);

3 + 42 = (7/4) related to 3 + 43 = (.........);

4 + 32 = (7/4 related to 4 + 33 = (.........).

AS IT CAN BE SEEN, THE BIG NUMBER INDICATES THE NUMBER OF MOVEMENTS IN THE TIME SIGNATURE; THE NUMBER 2 INDICATES THE TWO TONES OF THE BINARY RHYTHM, THE SMALL NUMBER INDICATES THE THREE TONES OF THE TRINARY RHYTHM. THE TWO BIG NUMBERS ADDED UP INDICATE THE DIFFERENT AND DISTINCT WAYS OF MARKING MIXED TIME SIGNATURES AND COMPOUNDED TIME SIGNATURES.
AT THE SAME TIME, THE HALFNOTE DEFINITELY AND INVARIABLY REPRESENTS THE MOVEMENT. AS A CONSEQUENCE, THE QUARTER NOTE WILL REPRESENT THE TONE AND THE EIGHTH NOTE THE SUBTONE.
THE TUPLET AND THE QUADRUPLET WILL THEREFORE INVARIABLY EXPRESS THE BINARY RHYTHM IN THE TRINARY MOVEMENT IN THE SAME WAY AS THE EQUIVALENT AND RELATIVE TRIPLETS AND SEXTUPLET WILL INVARIABLY EXPRESS THE TRINARY RHYTHM IN THE BINARY MOVEMENT.
5. WHILE THE RHYTHM UNFURLS, THE TONES, SUBTONES AND MOVEMENTS DEPEND FROM THE

RELATED TONES, SUBTONES AND PAUSES; THE SUBTONES OF THE PAUSES DEPEND FROM THE TONES OF PAUSE AND MOVEMENT; IN THE SAME WAY THE TONES OF PAUSES DEPEND FROM THE MOVEMENTS OF PAUSE AND MOVEMENT. IN ANY MEASURE OF TIME, BE IT BINARY, TRINARY, MIXED, SIMPLE OR COMPOUND, ALL THE MOVEMENTS, ALL THE TONES AND THE SUBTONES – OF PAUSE AND MOVEMENT – RELATIVELY DEPEND FROM THE MOVEMENT OF THE TONE AND FROM THE SUBTONE OF PAUSE OF THE TIME SIGNATURE.

The resulting equation is the ABSOLUTE SCIENTIFIC PRINCIPLE OF RHYTHM IN THE FORMULA : (1, 2, 3 and THEIR MULTIPLES) = (1 : 2 AND 3 AND THEIR MULTIPLES), and we now also have a PRACTICAL AND FUNCTIONAL WAY to CALCULATE IT in its most COMPLICATED, WHIMSICAL AND UNEXPECTED RELATIONS AND COMBINATIONS AN ARTIST MAY DISCOVER.

Yet this is not all; from THE THEORETICAL-PRACTICAL PRINCIPLE we must pass to the amazing results deriving from its conceptual and formal evolution.

Thanks to rhythm the human word teaches that its origins should be tracked down in singing, a primitive way of expression common to men and animals. The word retains indeed two values: THE INTELLECTUAL AND CONVENTIONAL VALUE AND THE EXPRESSIVE AND REAL VALUE. Therefore, its rhythm and articulation – since the word is a sort of ARTICULATED SONG – independently from its meaning, awake again in those who listen a sensation corresponding to that proved by the creator of the same word, through a similar state of mind. From here derives the MUSICAL (RHYTHMIC) value of poetry.

THE SUCCESSION OF TONES IN THE MUSICAL RHYTHM AND IN THE RHYTHM OF WORDS IS THE SAME, SINCE IT RELIES ON A SIMILAR PRINCIPLE.

In the following examples the syllables indicating a PAUSE (STRONG) are marked with a CIRCUMFLEX ACCENT, and the syllable indicating a MOVEMENT (WEAK) by an ACUTE ACCENT.

Binary rhythm.

Câr-né; têr-rà; mê-rá-mên-té; etc.
1 2 1 2 1 2 1 2
1 2

Vé-lô-cé; có-lô-ré; tém-pê-stá; etc.
1 2 1 2 1 2
2 2 2

Tû...; rê...; ciô...; etc.
1 2 1 2 1 2

^ tú; ^ ré; ^ ció; etc.
1 2 1 2 1 2

Trinary rhythm.

Fûl-gí-dó; ê-té-ró-gê-né-ó; â-gíta-nó; etc.
1 2 3 1 2 3 1 2 3 12
1 2 1 2 3

Ant-âr-tí-có; bé-vên-dó-sí; ér-bâ-cé-ó; etc.
1 2 3 1 2 3 1 2 3
2 2 2

Giô-vín...; vêr-gín...; câr-dín...; etc.
1 2 3 1 2 3 1 2 3

^ ‘ sí; ^ ‘ vá; ^ ‘ nó; etc.
1 2 3 1 2 3 1 2 3

Mixed rhythm.

Côn-té-stâ-bí-lé; sû-scét-tî-bí-lé; côm-mén-dê-vó-lé; etc.
1 2 1 2 3 1 2 1 2 3 1 2 1 2 3
1 2 1 2 1 2

Vâ-lí-dá-mên-té; â-stró-nó-mî-á; crî-só-bé-rîl-ló; etc.
1 2 3 1 2 1 2 3 1 2 1 2 3 1 2
1 2 1 2 1 2

Ar-tî-stí-cá-mên-té; é-lêt-tró-má-gnê-té; etc.
1 2 3 1 2 1 2 3 1 2
2 3 2 3

Có-rê-ó-grâ-fí-có; á-pô-cá-lît-tí-có; etc.
1 2 1 1 2 1 2 3
2 3 2 3

The dots under the accent indicate a PAUSE.
Towards the end of the Middle Ages, at the time of the troubadours, when a great tradition was on the verge of great transformations, next to religious and popular music there was

a third genre: THE MUSIC OF THE MIDDLE CLASSES.

This elegant, romantic and light genre, with its short compositions, was the perfect soundtrack for good digestion, lascivious loves, an amateur nobleman and a prince's house. It consisted indeed in short lounge music compositions, with frequent candences marking every period of a determined length.

These compositions spawned MONORHYTHMIC DANCE ROUTINES, SHORT ARIAS THAT INSPIRED THE MOVEMENTS OF DANCE STEPS and the preconception of the QUADRATURE IN THE COMPOSITION. From its inception, this virus spread throughout all the centuries, infecting music compositions even in our days.

The troubadours with good memory, love and joy of our famous LIBRETTISTS, treated poetry like a music; THIS must have happened contemporaneously since in those times poetry was never separated from music (SINGING); and probably it was for a RHYTHMIC-MUSICAL reason that verse lost its FIRST QUANTITATIVE METRE.

Terms such as SIRVENTESE, BALLAD, SONG, DANCE SONGS, SONNET and so on, appear both in music and poetry, with some references to the LITTLE SQUARE DANCES. The symmetrical and measured dance routines repeated with the same RHYTHM and the same CADENCES-RHYMES are also common to both these arts; DANTE'S POEM and BEETHOVEN's SYMPHONY are both subjected to the TIRANNY OF THE QUADRATURE OF THE MIDDLE CLASS DANCE. I'm not adding any comments about the others.

In poetry FREE VERSE marked the end of the slavery that let the INDIVIDUAL RHYTHM of the words – combined in symphonies of sounds and rhythms previously unheard of –

triumph.

In music Wagner, Strauss, Debussy and Mascagni's attempts did not solve the problem, even though they opened out new and different solutions.

Following Wagner's steps, Strauss turned the RECITATIVE PARTS INTO SYMPHONY, introducing time changes especially in those parts where the musical expression does not preserve the CONTINUATIVE MANNER; for this reason the effect was almost totally lost.

The same can be more or less said about all the others; by often applying changes in time signatures, they do not manage to offer any variety and absolute freedom to the RHYTHMIC THOUGHT.

Mascagni must be lauded for having understood the RHYTHMIC VALUE OF THE SUNG WORD and having applied it to his works with excellent results.

The introduction of the FREE RHYTHM IN MUSIC is a new conquest of futurism.

Before presenting our FINAL CONCLUSIONS; I would like to show how, through the rhythmic analysis of some FREE VERSES by poet Paolo Buzzi, the alternation of the binary and trinary rhythms and the formation of the mixed rhythms can be considered as an absolutely new RHYTHMIC LIBERTY and how between one verse and the other there isn't any SIMMETRY.

^...Nói siâm gli á-strâ-lí, ^... í sân-tí, ^...i dê-mó-nî-á-cí:

1 2 1 2 1 2 1 2 1 2 1 2 1 2 1 2 1

siam lé mé-tê-ó-ré vêr-tí-gí-nô-sé chiû-sé nell'â-tó-mó u-mâ-nó:

1 2 3 1 2 3 1 2 3 1 2 1 2 3 1 2

1 2 3

^...rí-pé-tiâ-mó, ^...frâ nói, ^...lé scôs-sé dê-gli ú-ní-vêr-sí fuô-rí dell'ôr-bí-té:

1 2 3 1 2 1 2 1 2 3 1 2 1 2 3 1 2 1 2 3 1 2 3

^...pró-pá-ghiâ-mó, ^...frâ nôi, ^...lá spê-cié déi cá-tâ-clî-smí êm-pí-ré-â-lí!

1 2 3 1 2 1 2 1 2 3 1 2 1 2 3 1 2 1 2 3 1 2

CONCLUSIONS:

1. FUTURIST MUSIC ACHIEVES AN ABSOLUTE FREEDOM OF RHYTHM BY EXPRESSING ITSELF THROUGH THE MULTIFORM VARIETY AND INDIVIDUAL INDEPENDENCE THAT THE FREE VERSE FOUND IN LITERATURE.

THE SENTENCE, MELODIC SYNTHESIS OF THE MUSICAL EXPRESSION – that can be composed of one or more time signatures – apart from assuming the rhythmic freedom of each time signature, can be enriched with new rhythmic movements by conceiving the time signatures that form it as DIFFERENT ONE FROM THE OTHER IN THE NUMBER OF MOVEMENTS AND IN THEIR RHYTHMS : BINARILY AND TRINARILY alternating BINARY, TRINARY AND MIXED TIME SIGNATURES IN ONE SENTENCE or let one follow the other.

2. THE MUSICAL PERIOD, FEATURING ONE OR MORE SENTENCES IN ITS FORMAL CONCEPTION MUST FOLLOW THE SAME PRINCIPLE OF FREEDOM AND VARIETY ALREADY ESTABLISHED FOR THE FORMATION OF THE SENTENCE : THAT IS BINARILY AND TRINARILY ALTERNATING SENTENCES THAT MAY BE THE SAME OR MAY BE DIFFERENT AMONG THEM FOR WHAT REGARDS THE NUMBER OR THE RHYTHM OF TIME SIGNATURES THAT MAKE THEM, OR LET ONE

FOLLOW THE OTHER.

3. THE SAME CAN BE SAID ABOUT THE BINARY AND TRINARY SUCCESSION AND ALTERNATION OF THE PERIODS, THAT MAKE UP IN THE SYMPHONY THE MELODIC MUSIC SYNTHESIS, A PREDOMINANTLY DESIRED EXPRESSION.

4. IN THIS WAY THE ENTIRE MUSICAL CONCEPTION IS SUMMARISED IN THE SCIENTIFIC FORMULA OF THE RHYTHM (1 X 2 AND THEIR MULTIPLES) = (1 : 2 AND 3 AND THEIR MULTIPLES) AND AT THE SAME TIME IT HAS FINALLY GOT THE FREEDOM TO DEVELOP THE FORMULA IN ALL THE POSSIBLE COMBINATIONS AND PROPORTIONS, ESTABLISHING THE FOLLOWING RELATIVE UNITS THAT CAN BE MULTIPLIED AND DIVIDED IN THE SAME WAY :

"SUBTONE – TONE – MOVEMENT – TIME SIGNATURE – SENTENCE – PERIOD – SYMPHONY".

In any case THE MOVEMEMT always represents THE CARDINAL RHYTHMIC UNIT.

5. THE QUADRATURE, WITH ITS SYMMETRIES AND CADENCES OF THE MIDDLE CLASS DANCE ROUTINES, IS DESTROYED AND SUBSTITUTED BY THE FREE INTUITION OF INSTINCTIVE AND JOYFUL RHYTHMIC RELATIONS.

6. ONCE THE CRITERIA OF STABLE TIME IS DESTROYED, ALSO THE USELESS TERMS ANDANTE, ALLEGRO, ALLEGRETTO, ETC ARE DESTROYED.

SUCH TERMS ARE SUBSTITUTED WITH A TERM THAT DESCRIBES THE MOOD IN WHICH THE CREATOR AND ARTIST FINDS HIMSELF AT THAT SPECIFIC MOMENT OF TIME.

We have definitely DESTROYED THE CENTURIES-OLD

QUADRATURE. Let's therefore celebrate FREE RHYTHM AND EXPRESSION; a rhythm as free as THE WORD, as free as the FUTURIST VERSE, a FLIGHT OF FANCY or the BEAT OF A HEART.

No conductor will therefore be able to subjugate the beats of a heart to the control of his BATON – AS MELANCHOLIC AND SLEEPY AS A PENDULUM CLOCK.

THE ORDER is an OLD POLICEMAN who doesn't have good legs to run; **WE, THE FUTURISTS ARE CREATING A NEW ORDER OF THE DISORDER.**

THE ART OF NOISES

LUIGI RUSSOLO

11 March 1913

Dear Balilla Pratella, great Futurist composer,

In Rome, in the Costanzi Theatre, packed to capacity, while I was listening to the orchestral performance of your overwhelming Futurist music, with my Futurist friends, Marinetti, Boccioni, Carrà, Balla, Soffici, Papini and Cavacchioli, a new art came into my mind which only you can create, the Art of Noises, the logical consequence of your marvelous innovations.

Ancient life was all silence. In the nineteenth century, with the invention of the machine, Noise was born. Today, Noise triumphs and reigns supreme over the sensibility of men. For many centuries life went by in silence, or at most in muted tones. The strongest noises which interrupted this silence were not intense or prolonged or varied. If we overlook such exceptional movements as earthquakes, hurricanes, storms, avalanches and waterfalls, nature is silent.

Amidst this dearth of noises, the first sounds that man drew from a pieced reed or streched string were regarded with amazement as new and marvelous things. Primitive races attributed sound to the gods; it was considered sacred and reserved for priests, who used it to enrich the mystery of their rites.

And so was born the concept of sound as a thing in

itself, distinct and independent of life, and the result was music, a fantastic world superimposed on the real one, an inviolatable and sacred world. It is easy to understand how such a concept of music resulted inevitable in the hindering of its progress by comparison with the other arts. The Greeks themselves, with their musical theories calculated mathematically by Pythagoras and according to which only a few consonant intervals could be used, limited the field of music considerably, rendering harmony, of which they were unaware, impossible.

The Middle Ages, with the development and modification of the Greek tetrachordal system, with the Gregorian chant and popular songs, enriched the art of music, but continued to consider sound in its development in time, a restricted notion, but one which lasted many centuries, and which still can be found in the Flemish contrapuntalists' most complicated polyphonies.

The chord did not exist, the development of the various parts was not subornated to the chord that these parts put together could produce; the conception of the parts was horizontal not vertical. The desire, search, and taste for a simultaneous union of different sounds, that is for the chord (complex sound), were gradually made manifest, passing from the consonant perfect chord with a few passing dissonances, to the complicated and persistent dissonances that characterize contemporary music.

At first the art of music sought purity, limpidity and sweetness of sound. Then different sounds were amalgamated, care being taken, however, to caress the ear with gentle harmonies. Today music, as it becomes continually more complicated, strives to amalgamate the most dissonant, strange and harsh sounds. In this way we come ever closer to noise-sound.

This musical evolution is paralleled by the multipication of machines, which collaborate with man on every front. Not only in the roaring atmosphere of major cities, but in the country too, which until yesterday was totally silent, the machine today has created such a variety and rivalry of noises that pure sound, in its exiguity and monotony, no longer arouses any feeling.

To excite and exalt our sensibilities, music developed towards the most complex polyphony and the maximum variety, seeking the most complicated successions of dissonant chords and vaguely preparing the creation of musical noise. This evolution towards "noise sound" was not possible before now. The ear of an eighteenth-century man could never have endured the discordant intensity of certain chords produced by our orchestras (whose members have trebled in number since then). To our ears, on the other hand, they sound pleasant, since our hearing has already been educated by modern life, so teeming with variegated noises. But our ears are not satisfied merely with this, and demand an abundance of acoustic emotions.

On the other hand, musical sound is too limited in its qualitative variety of tones. The most complex orchestras boil down to four or five types of instrument, varying in timber: instruments played by bow or plucking, by blowing into metal or wood, and by percussion. And so modern music goes round in this small circle, struggling in vain to create new ranges of tones.

This limited circle of pure sounds must be broken, and the infinite variety of "noise-sound" conquered.

Besides, everyone will acknowledge that all musical sound carries with it a development of sensations that are already familiar and exhausted, and which predispose the listener to boredom in spite of the efforts of all the innovatory musicians. We Futurists have deeply loved and enjoyed the harmonies of the great masters. For many years Beethoven and Wagner shook our nerves and hearts. Now we are satiated and we find far more enjoyment in the combination of the noises of trams, backfiring motors, carriages and bawling crowds than in rehearsing, for example, the "Eroica" or the "Pastoral".

We cannot see that enormous apparatus of force that the modern orchestra represents without feeling the most profound and total disillusion at the paltry acoustic results. Do you know of any sight more ridiculous than that of twenty men furiously bent on the redoubling the mewing of a violin? All this will naturally make the music-lovers scream, and will perhaps enliven the sleepy atmosphere of concert halls. Let us now, as Futurists, enter one of these hospitals for anaemic sounds. There: the first bar brings the boredom of familiarity to your ear and anticipates the boredom of the bar to follow. Let us relish, from bar to bar, two or three varieties of genuine boredom, waiting all the while for the extraordinary sensation that never comes.

Meanwhile a repugnant mixture is concocted from monotonous sensations and the idiotic religious emotion of listeners buddhistically drunk with repeating for the nth time their more or less snobbish or second-hand ecstasy.

Away! Let us break out since we cannot much longer restrain our desire to create finally a new musical reality, with a generous distribution of resonant slaps in the face, discarding violins, pianos, double-basses and plainitive organs. Let us break out!

It's no good objecting that noises are exclusively loud and disagreeable to the ear.

It seems pointless to enumerate all the graceful and

delicate noises that afford pleasant sensations.

To convince ourselves of the amazing variety of noises, it is enough to think of the rumble of thunder, the whistle of the wind, the roar of a waterfall, the gurgling of a brook, the rustling of leaves, the clatter of a trotting horse as it draws into the distance, the lurching jolts of a cart on pavings, and of the generous, solemn, white breathing of a nocturnal city; of all the noises made by wild and domestic animals, and of all those that can be made by the mouth of man without resorting to speaking or singing.

Let us cross a great modern capital with our ears more alert than our eyes, and we will get enjoyment from distinguishing the eddying of water, air and gas in metal pipes, the grumbling of noises that breathe and pulse with indisputable animality, the palpitation of valves, the coming and going of pistons, the howl of mechanical saws, the jolting of a tram on its rails, the cracking of whips, the flapping of curtains and flags. We enjoy creating mental orchestrations of the crashing down of metal shop blinds, slamming doors, the hubbub and shuffling of crowds, the variety of din, from stations, railways, iron foundries, spinning wheels, printing works, electric power stations and underground railways.

Nor should the newest noises of modern war be forgotten. Recently, the poet Marinetti, in a letter from the trenches of Adrianopolis, described to me with marvelous free words the orchestra of a great battle:

"every 5 seconds siege cannons gutting space with a chord ZANG-TUMB-TUUMB mutiny of 500 echos smashing scattering it to infinity. In the center of this hateful ZANG-TUMB-TUUMB area 50square kilometers leaping bursts lacerations fists rapid fire batteries. Violence ferocity regularity this deep bass scanning

the strange shrill frantic crowds of the battle Fury breathless ears eyes nostrils open! load! fire! what a joy to hear to smell completely taratatata of the machine guns screaming a breathless under the stings slaps traak-traak whips pic-pac-pum-tumb weirdness leaps 200 meters range Far far in back of the orchestra pools muddying huffing goaded oxen wagons pluff-plaff horse action flic flac zing zing shaaack laughing whinnies the tiiinkling jiiingling tramping 3 Bulgarian battalions marching croooc-craaac [slowly] Shumi Maritza or Karvavena ZANG-TUMB-TUUUMB toc-toc-toc-toc [fast] crooc-craac [slowly] crys of officers slamming about like brass plates pan here paak there BUUUM ching chaak [very fast] cha-cha-cha-cha-chaak down there up around high up look out your head beautiful! Flashing flashing flashing flashing flashing flashing footlights of the forts down there behind that smoke Shukri Pasha communicates by phone with 27 forts in Turkish in German Allo! Ibrahim! Rudolf! allo! allo! actors parts echos of prompters scenery of smoke forests applause odor of hay mud dung I no longer feel my frozen feet odor of gunsmoke odor of rot Tympani flutes clarinets everywhere low high birds chirping blessed shadows cheep-cheep-cheep green breezes flocks don-dan-don-din-baaah Orchestra madmen pommel the performers they terribly beaten playing Great din not erasing clearing up cutting off slighter noises very small scraps of echos in the theater area 300 square kilometers Rivers Maritza Tungia stretched out Rodolpi Mountains rearing heights loges boxes 2000 shrapnels waving arms exploding very white handkerchiefs full of gold srrrr-TUMB-TUMB 2000 raised grenades tearing out bursts of very black hair ZANG-srrrr-TUMB-ZANG-TUMB-TUUMB the orchestra of the noises of war swelling under a held note of silence in the high sky round golden balloon that observes the firing..."

We want to attune and regulate this tremendous variety of noises harmonically and rhythmically.

To attune noises does not mean to detract from all their irregular movements and vibrations in time and intensity, but rather to give gradation and tone to the most strongly predominant of these vibrations.

Noise in fact can be differentiated from sound only in so far as the vibrations which produce it are confused and irregular, both in time and intensity.

Every noise has a tone, and sometimes also a harmony that predominates over the body of its irregular vibrations.

Now, it is from this dominating characteristic tone that a practical possibility can be derived for attuning it, that is to give a certain noise not merely one tone, but a variety of tones, without losing its characteristic tone, by which I mean the one which distinguishes it. In this way any noise obtained by a rotating movement can offer an entire ascending or descending chromatic scale, if the speed of the movement is increased or decreased.

Every manifestation of our life is accompanied by noise. The noise, therefore, is familiar to our ear, and has the power to conjure up life itself. Sound, alien to our life, always musical and a thing unto itself, an occasional but unnecessary element, has become to our ears what an overfamiliar face is to our eyes. Noise, however, reaching us in a confused and irregular way from the irregular confusion of our life, never entirely reveals itself to us, and keeps innumerable surprises in reserve. We are therefore certain that by selecting, coordinating and dominating all noises we will enrich men with a new and unexpected sensual pleasure.

Although it is characteristic of noise to recall us brutally to real life, the art of noise must not limit itself to imitative reproduction. It will achieve its most emotive power in the acoustic enjoyment, in its own right, that the artist's inspiration will extract from combined noises.

Here are the 6 families of noises of the Futurist orchestra which we will soon set in motion mechanically:

1

Rumbles
Roars
Explosions
Crashes
Splashes
Booms

2

Whistles
Hisses
Snorts

3

Whispers
Murmurs
Mumbles
Grumbles
Gurgles

4

Screeches
Creaks
Rumbles
Buzzes
Crackles
Scrapes

5

Noises obtained by percussion on metal, wood, skin, stone, tarracotta, etc.

6

Voices of animals and men:
Shouts
Screams
Groans
Shrieks
Howls
Laughs
Weezes
Sobs

In this inventory we have encapsulated the most characteristic of the fundamental noises; the others are merely the associations and combinations of these. The rhythmic movements of a noise are infinite: just as with tone there is always a predominant rhythm, but around this numerous other secondary rhythms can be felt.

Conclusions:

1. Futurist musicians must continually enlarge and enrich the field of sounds. This corresponds to a need in our sensibility. We note, in fact, in the composers of genius, a tendency towards the most complicated dissonances. As these move further and further away from pure sound, they almost achieve noise-sound. This need and this tendency cannot be satisfied except by the adding and the substitution of noises for sounds.

2. Futurist musicians must substitute for the limited variety of tones posessed by orchestral instruments today the infinite variety of tones of noises, reproduced with appropriate mechanisms.

3. The musician's sensibility, liberated from facile and traditional Rhythm, must find in noises the means of extension and renewal, given that every noise offers the union of the most diverse rhythms apart from the predominant one.

4. Since every noise contains a predominant general tone in its irregular vibrations it will be easy to obtain in the construction of instruments which imitate them a sufficiently extended variety of tones, semitones, and quarter-tones. This variety of tones will not remove the characteristic tone from each noise, but will amplify only its texture or extension.

5. The practical difficulties in constructing these instruments are not serious. Once the mechanical principle which produces the noise has been found, its

tone can be changed by following the same general laws of acoustics. If the instrument is to have a rotating movement, for instance, we will increase or decrease the speed, whereas if it is to not have rotating movement the noise-producing parts will vary in size and tautness.

6. The new orchestra will achieve the most complex and novel aural emotions not by incorporating a succession of life-imitating noises but by manipulating fantastic juxtapositions of these varied tones and rhythms. Therefore an instrument will have to offer the possibility of tone changes and varying degrees of amplification.

7. The variety of noises is infinite. If today, when we have perhaps a thousand different machines, we can distinguish a thousand different noises, tomorrow, as new machines multiply, we will be able to distinguish ten, twenty, or thirty thousand different noises, not merely in a simply imitative way, but to combine them according to our imagination.

8. We therefore invite young musicians of talent to conduct a sustained observation of all noises, in order to understand the various rhythms of which they are composed, their principal and secondary tones. By comparing the various tones of noises with those of sounds, they will be convinced of the extent to which the former exceed the latter. This will afford not only an understanding, but also a taste and passion for noises. After being conquered by Futurist eyes our multiplied sensibilities will at last hear with Futurist ears. In this way the motors and machines of our industrial cities will

one day be consciously attuned, so that every factory will be transformed into an intoxicating orchestra of noises.

Dear Pratella, I submit these statements to your Futurist genius, inviting your discussion. I am not a musician, I have therefore no acoustical predilictions, nor any works to defend. I am a Futurist painter using a much loved art to project my determination to renew everything. And so, bolder than a professional musician could be, unconcerned by my apparent incompetence and convinced that all rights and possibilities open up to daring, I have been able to initiate the great renewal of music by means of the Art of Noises.

THE FUTURIST NOISE MACHINES

LUIGI RUSSOLO

11 June 1913

On June 2, at a Futurist evening in Modena before 2,000 people who overcrowded the Teatro Stocchi, I explained and demonstrated one of the first *intonarumori* ("noise machines') – instruments invented and constructed by me in collaboration with the painter, Ugo Piatti. The perfect function of this apparatus or instrument (that has the special name of exploder), reproducing by a series of 10 whole tones the characteristic noise of a motor starting up, provoked violent enthusiasm and at the same time – like everything about our forceful movement – infinite discussions, and, naturally, bursts of imbecile or superficial laughter.

After having read numerous and diverse comments about the "Art of Noise" (March 11, 1913) that have been published principally by foreign newspapers – from Temps to Matin, from Berliner Tageblatt to Neues Wiener, from the Daily Chronicle to the Evening Standard I was persuaded that all these newspapers have not understood in its essence, however clearly enunciated, the intuitive principle of that manifesto, and what should have been the practical realisation that must have been logically derived from the principle.

Several – the major part – have imagined only a cacophony as a practical result; a deafening and disorderly medley of noise without sense or any logic; others have imagined a simple imitative or impressionistic intention to copy the noises of life. Lastly, others have seen in that manifesto only the desire to launch sentences and snobbish theories to amaze the good bourgeoisie.

All this, naturally, did not discourage me and it also did not hide from me the many and grave difficulties that must be overcome in order to arrive at a practical realisation of the manifesto. I continued to work and to do research on the subject.

If from afar I heard and still hear laughter, jokes, or expressions of incredulity about my idea, near me, instead, I have had and have among my old and new Futurist brothers an atmosphere of rousing enthusiasm.

I will point, first of all, to the enthusiasm and to the inexhaustible young faith of that great animator who is my dear and great friend, Marinetti, who is still vibrating from the great acoustic emotion of his experience assisting in the siege of Adrianople.

In my long and patient laboratory research I have had and I have a faithful companion, an ingenious and untiring researcher, the painter Ugo Piatti.

What I said in the manifesto, "We want to intone and regulate harmonically and rhythmically these extremely varied noises," is today a reality, and the instruments that realised the "intoned noises" are, by now, incessantly multiplying them.

Without going into the particular techniques, I shall briefly point out the practical results already obtained and those that are deemed to be possible in a short time by already completed studies.

Acoustics has taught us very little, since, having been applied to the study of pure sounds until now, it has almost completely neglected the study of noise.

Except for several general laws on sounds that also serve

in part for noise, acoustics had to proceed almost uniquely by means of continual and repeated experiments.

Above all, it was necessary for practicability for these intonarumori instruments to be of the greatest simplicity possible and it is this, exactly, that we have succeeded in perfectly.

It is enough to say that a single taut diaphragm suitably placed gives, by variation of its tension, a gamut of more than 10 whole tones, with all the passages of semitones, of quarter-tones and also smaller fractions of tones.

The preparation of the material for this diaphragm by means of special chemical baths varies according to the timbre of noise that one wishes to obtain. Then, by varying the means of excitation of the same diaphragm, one also can obtain a different noise, in type and in timbre, always preserving, naturally, the possibility of varying the tone. There are four different means of excitation used before now and the corresponding instruments have already been completed.

The first gives the sound of exploding, automobile-motor type; the second gives a crackling sound, the fusillade type; the third gives a humming sound, the dynamic type; the fourth gives the sound of different varieties of rubbing.

In these instruments it is enough that the simple shifting of a graduated lever gives the tone of noise that one wants, also its smallest fraction. The rhythm of every single noise can also be equally regulated, so one can easily calculate in bars the even and uneven tempos that exist.

These instruments, because of their extreme simplicity, are already perfect enough so that they need only small modifications of a secondary nature.

The research to obtain noises (always, it is well understood, tuneable) of the first series listed in the manifesto is now already complete: the "Roars," "Thunders," and the "Bursts"; of the second series: the "Hisses"; of the third: the "Bubblings"; of the fourth: the "Screeches" and the "Rustles." The relative instruments for these noises are already in execution: the "Roarer," "Thunderer," "Burster," and the "Bubbler."

And now I shall say some words about the effects that noises thus intoned produce on those who listen. As I pointed out in the manifesto, noise that comes from life we immediately restore to the same life (contrary to that which makes the sound) reminiscing quickly in our minds about the things that produce the determined noise that we hear. The restoration to life has, therefore, a character of an impressionistic fragmented episode of the same life. But as in every art, and thus also in the Art of Noise, we must not limit ourselves to an impressionistic fragmented reproduction of life. Noise must become a primary element in shaping the work of art. That is, it must lose its own accidental character in order to become an element sufficiently abstract so that it can reach the necessary transfiguration of every primary element in the abstract material of art.

Well then, although the resemblance of timbre to imitated natural noise is attained in these instruments, almost to the point of misleading, nevertheless, as soon as one hears that noise varies in tone, one becomes aware that it quickly loses its episodic, uniquely imitative character. It loses, that is, all its character of result and effect, tied to causes that produce it (motor energy, percussions, rubbings produced by speed, clashes, etc.) and that are due to and inherent in the same purpose of the machine or of some other thing that produces the noise.

It loses this character of effect by transforming itself into element and into primary material.

And when noise is thus liberated from the things that produce it we dominate it, transforming it into our desired tone, intensity, and rhythm; we hear noise quickly become automatic material, malleable, ready to be shaped by the wishes of the artist who transforms it into an element of emotion, into a work of art.

And it is thus that choosing, dominating, and co-ordinating noises, we have already in part reached that new unexpected delight of which we spoke in the manifesto *The Art Of Noises*.

APPENDIX

SKETCH FOR A NEW AESTHETIC OF SOUND ART

FERRUCCIO BUSONI

1906

"What seek you? Say! And what do you expect?"– "I know not what; the Unknown I would have! What's known to me, is endless; I would go Beyond the end: The last word still is wanting."

–*Der mächtige Zauberer.*

Loosely joined together as regards literary form, the following notes are, in reality, the outcome of convictions long held and slowly matured.

In them a problem of the first magnitude is formulated with apparent simplicity, without giving the key to its final solution; for the problem cannot be solved for generations – if at all.

But it involves an innumerable series of lesser problems, which I present to the consideration of those whom they may concern. For it is a long time since any one has devoted himself to earnest musical research.

It is true, that admirable works of genius arise in every period, and I have always taken my stand in the front rank of those who joyfully acclaimed the passing standard-bearers; and still it seems to me that of all these beautiful paths leading so far afield – none lead *upward.*

The spirit of an art-work, the measure of emotion, of

humanity, that is in it – these remain unchanged in value through changing years; the form which these three assumed, the manner of their expression, and the flavor of the epoch which gave them birth, are transient, and age rapidly.

Spirit and emotion retain their essence, in the art-work as in man himself; we admire technical achievements, yet they are outstripped, or cloy the taste and are discarded.
Its ephemeral qualities give a work the stamp of "modernity;" its unchangeable essence hinders it from becoming "obsolete." Among both "modern" and "old" works we find good and bad, genuine and spurious. There is nothing properly modern – only things which have come into being earlier or later; longer in bloom, or sooner withered. The Modern and the Old have always been.

Art-forms are the more lasting, the more closely they adhere to the nature of their individual species of art, the purer they keep their essential means and ends.

Sculpture relinquishes the expression of the human pupil, and effects of color; painting degenerates, when it forsakes the flat surface in depiction and takes on complexity in theatrical decoration or panoramic portrayal.

Architecture has its fundamental form, growth from below upward, prescribed by static necessity; window and roof necessarily provide the intermediate and finishing configuration; these are eternal and inviolable requirements of the art.

Poetry commands the abstract thought, which it clothes in words. More independent than the others, it reaches the furthest bounds.

But all arts, resources and forms ever aim at the one end, namely, the imitation of nature and the interpretation of human feelings.

Architecture, sculpture, poetry and painting are old and mature arts; their conceptions are established and their objects assured; they have found the way through uncounted centuries, and, like the planets, describe their regular orbits.[1]

Music, compared with them, is a child that has learned to walk, but must still be led. It is a virgin art, without experience in life and suffering.

It is all unconscious as yet of what garb is becoming, of its own advantages, its unawakened capacities. And again, it is a child-marvel that is already able to dispense much of beauty, that has already brought joy to many, and whose gifts are commonly held to have attained full maturity.

Music as an art, our so-called occidental music, is hardly four hundred years old; its state is one of development, perhaps the very first stage of a development beyond present conception, and we – we talk of "classics" and "hallowed traditions"! And we have talked of them for a long time![2]

We have formulated rules, stated principles, laid down laws; – we apply laws made for maturity to a child that knows nothing of responsibility!

Young as it is, this child, we already recognize that it possesses one radiant attribute which signalizes it beyond all its elder sisters. And the lawgivers will not see this marvelous attribute, lest their laws should be thrown to the winds. This child – it *floats on air*! It touches not the earth with its feet. It knows no law of gravitation. It is wellnigh incorporeal. Its material is transparent. It is sonorous air. It is almost Nature herself. It is – free.

But freedom is something that mankind have never wholly

comprehended, never realized to the full. They can neither recognize nor acknowledge it.

They disavow the mission of this child; they hang weights upon it. This buoyant creature must walk decently, like anybody else. It may scarcely be allowed to leap – when it were its joy to follow the line of the rainbow, and to break sunbeams with the clouds.

Music was born free; and to win freedom is its destiny. It will become the most complete of all reflexes of Nature by reason of its untrammeled immateriality. Even the poetic word ranks lower in point of incorporealness. It can gather together and disperse, can be motionless repose or wildest tempestuosity; it has the extremest heights perceptible to man – what other art has these? – and its emotion seizes the human heart with that intensity which is independent of the "idea."

It realizes a temperament, *without* describing it, with the mobility of the soul, with the swiftness of consecutive moments; and this, where painter or sculptor can represent only one side or one moment, and the poet tardily *communicates* a temperament and its manifestations by words.

Therefore, representation and description are not the nature of music; herewith we declare the invalidity of program-music, and arrive at the question: What are the aims of music?

Absolute Music! What the lawgivers mean by this, is perhaps remotest of all from the Absolute in music. "Absolute music" is a form-play without poetic program, in which the form is intended to have the leading part. But Form, in itself, is the opposite pole of absolute music, on which was bestowed the divine prerogative of buoyancy, of freedom from the limitations of matter. In a picture, the illustration of a sunset ends with the frame; the limitless natural phenomenon is enclosed in quadrilateral bounds; the cloud-form chosen for depiction remains unchanging for ever. Music can grow brighter or darker, shift hither or yon, and finally fade away like the sunset glow itself; and instinct leads the creative musician to employ the tones that press the same key within the human breast, and awaken the same response, as the processes in Nature.

Per contra, "absolute music" is something very sober, which reminds one of music-desks in orderly rows, of the relation of Tonic to Dominant, of Developments and Codas.

Methinks I hear the second violin struggling, a fourth below, to emulate the more dexterous first, and contending in needless contest merely to arrive at the starting-point. This sort of music ought rather to be called the "architectonic," or "symmetric," or "sectional," and derives from the circumstance that certain composers poured *their* spirit and *their* emotion into just this mould as lying nearest them or their time. Our lawgivers have identified the spirit and emotion, the individuality of these composers and their time, with "symmetric" music, and finally, being powerless to recreate either the spirit, or the emotion, or the time, have retained the Form as a symbol, and made it into a fetish, a religion. The composers sought and found this form as the aptest vehicle for communicating *their* ideas; their souls took flight – and the lawgivers discover and cherish the garments Euphorion left behind on earth.

A lucky find! 'Twas now or never; The flame is gone, it's true – however, No need to pity mankind now. Enough is left for many a poet's tiring, Or to breed envy high and low; And though I have no talents here for hiring, I'll hire the robe out, anyhow.

Is it not singular, to demand of a composer originality

in all things, and to forbid it as regards form? No wonder that, once he becomes original, he is accused of "formlessness." Mozart! the seeker and the finder, the great man with the childlike heart – it is he we marvel at, to whom we are devoted; but not his Tonic and Dominant, his Developments and Codas.

Such lust of liberation filled Beethoven, the romantic revolutionary, that he ascended one short step on the way leading music back to its loftier self: – a short step in the great task, a wide step in his own path. He did not quite reach absolute music, but in certain moments he divined it, as in the introduction to the fugue of the Sonata for Hammerclavier. Indeed, all composers have drawn nearest the true nature of music in preparatory and intermediary passages (preludes and transitions), where they felt at liberty to disregard symmetrical proportions, and unconsciously drew free breath. Even a Schumann (of so much lower stature) is seized, in such passages, by some feeling of the boundlessness of this pan-art (recall the transition to the last movement of the D-minor Symphony); and the same may be asserted of Brahms in the introduction to the Finale of his First Symphony.

But, the moment they cross the threshold of the *Principal Subject*, their attitude becomes stiff and conventional, like that of a man entering some bureau of high officialdom.

Next to Beethoven, Bach bears closest affinity to "infinite music." His Organ Fantasias (but not the Fugues) have indubitably a strong dash of what might be overwritten "Man and Nature."[3] In him it appears most ingenuous because he had no reverence for his predecessors (although he esteemed and made use of them), and because the still novel acquisition of equal temperament opened a vista of – for the time being –

endless new possibilities.

Therefore, Bach and Beethoven[4] are to be conceived as a *beginning*, and not as unsurpassable finalities. In spirit and emotion they will probably remain unexcelled; and this, again, confirms the remark at the beginning of these lines: That spirit and emotion remain unchanged in value through changing years, and that he who mounts to their uttermost heights will always tower above the crowd.

What still remains to be surpassed, is their form of expression and their freedom. Wagner, a Germanic Titan, who touched our earthly horizon in orchestral tone-effect, who intensified the form of expression, but fashioned it into a *system* (music-drama, declamation, leading-motive), is on this account incapable of further intensification. His category begins and ends with himself; first, because he carried it to the highest perfection and finish; secondly, because his self-imposed task was of such a nature, that it could be achieved by one man alone.[5] The paths opened by Beethoven can be followed to their end only through generations. They – like all things in creation – may form only a circle; but a circle of such dimensions, that the portion visible to us seems like a straight line. Wagner's circle we can view in its entirety – a circle within the great circle.

The name of Wagner leads to program-music. This has been set up as a contrast to so-called "absolute" music, and these concepts have become so petrified that even persons of intelligence hold one or the other dogma, without recognition for a third possibility beyond and above the other two. In reality, program-music is precisely as one-sided and limited as that which is called absolute. In place of architectonic and symmetric formulas, instead of the relation of Tonic to

Dominant, it has bound itself in the stays of a connecting poetic – sometimes even philosophic – program.

Every motive – so it seems to me – contains, like a seed, its life-germ within itself. From the different plant-seeds grow different families of plants, dissimilar in form, foliage, blossom, fruit, growth and color.[6]

Even each individual plant belonging to one and the same species assumes, in size, form and strength, a growth peculiar to itself. And so, in each motive, there lies the embryo of its fully developed form; each one must unfold itself differently, yet each obediently follows the law of eternal harmony. *This form is imperishable, though each be unlike every other.*

The motive in a composition with program bears within itself the same natural necessity; but it must, even in its earliest phase of development, renounce *its own proper mode of growth* to mould – or, rather, twist – itself to fit the needs of the program. Thus turned aside, at the outset, from the path traced by nature, it finally arrives at a wholly unexpected climax, whither it has been led, not by its own organization, but by the way laid down in the program, or the action, or the philosophical idea.

And how primitive must this art remain! True, there are unequivocal descriptive effects of tone-painting (from these the entire principle took its rise), but these means of expression are few and trivial, covering but a very small section of musical art. Begin with the most self-evident of all, the debasement of Tone to Noise in imitating the sounds of Nature – the rolling of thunder, the roar of forests, the cries of animals; then those somewhat less evident, symbolic – imitations of visual impressions, like the lightning-flash, springing movement, the flight of birds; again, those intelligible only through the mediation of the reflective brain, such as the trumpet-call as a warlike symbol, the shawm to betoken ruralism, march-rhythm to signify measured strides, the chorale as vehicle for religious feeling. Add to the above the characterization of nationalities – national instruments and airs – and we have a complete inventory of the arsenal of program-music. Movement and repose, minor and major, high and low, in their customary significance, round out the list. – These are auxiliaries, of which good use can be made upon a broad canvas, but which, taken by themselves, are no more to be called music than wax figures may pass for monuments.

And, after all, what can the presentation of a little happening upon this earth, the report concerning an annoying neighbor – no matter whether in the next room or in an adjoining quarter of the globe – have in common with that music which pervades the universe?

To music, indeed, it is given to set in vibration our human moods: Dread (*Leporello*), oppression of soul, invigoration, lassitude (Beethoven's last Quartets), decision (*Wotan*), hesitation, despondency, encouragement, harshness, tenderness, excitement, tranquillization, the feeling of surprise or expectancy, and still others; likewise the inner echo of external occurrences which is bound up in these moods of the soul. But not the moving cause itself of these spiritual affections; – not the joy over an avoided danger, not the danger itself, or the kind of danger which caused the dread; an emotional state, yes, but not the psychic species of this emotion, such as envy, or jealousy; and it is equally futile to attempt the expression, through music, of moral characteristics (vanity, cleverness), or abstract ideas like truth and justice. Is it possible to imagine how a poor, but contented man could be represented by music? The contentment, the soul-state, can be interpreted by music; but where does the poverty appear, or the important ethic problem stated in the words "poor, but contented"? This is due to the fact that "poor" connotes a phase of terrestrial and social conditions not to be found in the eternal harmony. And Music is a part of the vibrating universe.

I may be allowed to subjoin a few subsidiary reflections: – The greater part of modern theatre music suffers from the mistake of seeking to repeat the scenes passing on the stage, instead of fulfilling its own proper mission of interpreting the soul-states of the persons represented. When the scene presents the illusion of a thunderstorm, this is exhaustively apprehended by the eye. Nevertheless, nearly all composers strive to depict the storm in tones – which is not only a needless and feebler repetition, but likewise a failure to perform their true function. The person on the stage is either psychically influenced by the thunderstorm, or his mood, being absorbed in a train of thought of stronger influence, remains unaffected. The storm is visible and audible without aid from music; it is the invisible and inaudible, the spiritual processes of the personages portrayed, which music should render intelligible.

Again, there are "obvious" psychic conditions on the stage, whereof music need take no account. Suppose a theatrical situation in which a convivial company is passing at night and disappears from view, while in the foreground a silent, envenomed duel is in progress. Here the music, by means of continuing song, should keep in mind the jovial company now lost to sight; the acts and feelings of the pair in the foreground may be understood without further commentary, and the music

– dramatically speaking – ought not to participate in their action and break the tragic silence.

Measurably justified, in my opinion, is the plan of the old opera, which concentrated and musically rounded out the passions aroused by a moving dramatic scene in a piece of set form (the aria). *Word* and stage-play conveyed the dramatic progress of the action, followed more or less meagrely by musical recitative; arrived at the point of rest, music resumed the reins. This is less extrinsic than some would now have us believe. On the other hand, it was the ossified form of the "aria" itself which led to inveracity of expression and decadence.

The audible presentation, the "performance," of music, its *emotional interpretation*, derives from those free heights whence descended the Art itself. Where the art is threatened by earthliness, it is the part of interpretation to raise it and reëndow it with its primordial essence.

Notation, the writing out of compositions, is primarily an ingenious expedient for catching an inspiration, with the purpose of exploiting it later. But notation is to improvisation as the portrait to the living model. It is for the interpreter to *resolve the rigidity of the signs* into the primitive emotion.

But the lawgivers require the interpreter to reproduce the rigidity of the signs; they consider his reproduction the nearer to perfection, the more closely it clings to the signs.

What the composer's inspiration *necessarily* loses[7] through notation, his interpreter should restore by his own.

To the lawgivers, the signs themselves are the most important matter, and are continually growing in their estimation; the new art of music is derived from the old signs – *and these now stand for musical art itself.*

If the lawgivers had their way, any given composition

would always be reproduced in precisely the same tempo, whensoever, by whomsoever, and under whatsoever conditions it might be performed.

But, it *is* not possible; the buoyant, expansive nature of the divine child rebels – it demands the opposite. Each day begins differently from the preceding, yet always with the flush of dawn. – Great artists play their own works differently at each repetition, remodel them on the spur of the moment, accelerate and retard, in a way which they could not indicate by signs – and always according to the given conditions of that "eternal harmony."

And then the lawgiver chafes, and refers the creator to his own handwriting. As matters stand to-day, the lawgiver has the best of the argument.

"Notation" ("writing down") brings up the subject of Transcription, nowadays a term much misunderstood, almost discreditable. The frequent antagonism which I have excited with "transcriptions," and the opposition to which an ofttimes irrational criticism has provoked me, caused me to seek a clear understanding of this point. My final conclusion concerning it is this: Every notation is, in itself, the transcription of an abstract idea. The instant the pen seizes it, the idea loses its original form. The very intention to write down the idea, compels a choice of measure and key. The form, and the musical agency, which the composer must decide upon, still more closely define the way and the limits.

It is much the same as with man himself. Born naked, and as yet without definite aspirations, he decides, or at a given moment is made to decide, upon a career. From the moment of decision, although much that is original and imperishable in the idea or the man may live on, either is depressed to the type of a class. The musical idea becomes a sonata or a concerto; the man, a soldier or a priest. That is an Arrangement of the original. From this first transcription to a second the step is comparatively short and unimportant. And yet it is only the second, in general, of which any notice is taken; overlooking the fact, that a transcription does not destroy the archetype, which is, therefore, not lost through transcription.

Again, the performance of a work is also a transcription, and still, whatever liberties it may take, it can never annihilate the original.

For the musical art-work exists, before its tones resound and after they die away, *complete and intact.* It exists both within and outside of time, and through its nature we can obtain a definite conception of the otherwise intangible notion of the Ideality of Time.

For the rest, most of Beethoven's piano compositions sound like transcriptions of orchestral works; most of Schumann's orchestral compositions, like arrangements from pieces for the piano – and they are so, in a way.

Strangely enough, the Variation-Form is highly esteemed by the Worshippers of the Letter. That is singular; for the variation-form – when built up on a borrowed theme – produces a *whole series of "arrangements"* which, besides, are least respectful when most ingenious.

So the arrangement is *not* good, because it *varies* the original; and the variation *is* good, although it "*arranges*" the original.

The term "musikalisch" (musical) is used by the Germans in a sense foreign to that in which any other language employs it. It is a conception belonging to the Germans, and not to culture in general; the expression is incorrect and untranslatable. "Musical" is derived from *music*, like "poetical" from *poetry*, or "physical" from *physic(s)*. When I say, "Schubert was one of the most musical among men," it is the same as if I should say, "Helmholtz was one of the most physical among men." That is musical, which *sounds* in rhythms and intervals. A cupboard can be "musical," if "music-works" be enclosed in it.[8] In a comparative sense, "musical" may have the further signification of "euphonious." – "My verses are too musical to bear setting to music," a noted poet once remarked to me.

"Spirits moving musically
To a lute's well-tuned law,"

writes Edgar Allan Poe. Lastly, one may speak quite correctly of "musical laughter," because it *sounds* like music.

Taking the signification in which the term is applied and almost exclusively employed in German, a musical person is one who manifests an inclination for music by a nice discrimination and sensitiveness with regard to the *technical aspects* of the art. By "technics" I mean rhythm, harmony, intonation, part-leading, and the treatment of themes. The more subtleties he is capable of hearing or reproducing in these, the more "musical" he is held to be.

In view of the great importance attached to these elements of the art, this "musical" temperament has naturally become of the highest consequence. And so an artist who plays with perfect technical finish should be deemed the most musical player. But as we mean by "technics" only the mechanical mastery of the instrument, the terms "technical" and "musical" have been turned into opposites.

The matter has been carried so far as to call a

composition itself "musical,"[9] or even to assert of a great composer like Berlioz that he was not sufficiently musical.[10] "Unmusical" conveys the strongest reproach; branded thus, its object becomes an outlaw.[11]

In a country like Italy, where all participate in the delights of music, this differentiation becomes superfluous, and the term corresponding is not found in the language. In France, where a living sense of music does not permeate the people, there are musicians and non-musicians; of the rest, some "are very fond of music," and others "do not care for it." Only in Germany is it made a point of honor to be "musical," that is to say, not merely to love music, but more especially to understand it as regards its technical means of expression, and to obey their rules.

A thousand hands support the buoyant child and solicitously attend its footsteps, that it may not soar aloft where there might be risk of a serious fall. But it is still so young, and is eternal; the day of its freedom will come. – When it shall cease to be "musical."

The creator should take over no traditional law in blind belief, which would make him view his own creative endeavor, from the outset, as an exception contrasting with that law. For his individual case he should seek out and formulate a fitting individual law, which, after the first complete realization, he should annul, that he himself may not be drawn into repetitions when his next work shall be in the making.

The function of the creative artist consists in making laws, not in following laws ready made. He who follows such laws, ceases to be a creator.

Creative power may be the more readily recognized, the more it shakes itself loose from tradition. But an intentional avoidance of the rules cannot masquerade as creative power, and still less engender it.

The true creator strives, in reality, after *perfection* only. And through bringing this into harmony with *his own* individuality, a new law arises without premeditation.

So narrow has our tonal range become, so stereotyped its form of expression, that nowadays there is not one familiar motive that cannot be fitted with some other familiar motive so that the two may be played simultaneously. Not to lose my way in trifling,[12] I shall refrain from giving examples.

That which, within our present-day music, most nearly approaches the essential nature of the art, is the Rest and the Hold (Pause). Consummate players, improvisers, know how to employ these instruments of expression in loftier and ampler measure. The tense silence between two movements – *in itself music*, in this environment – leaves wider scope for divination than the more determinate, but therefore less elastic, sound.

What we now call our Tonal System is nothing more than a set of "signs"; an ingenious device to grasp somewhat of that eternal harmony; a meagre pocket-edition of that encyclopedic work; artificial light instead of the sun. – Have you ever noticed how people gaze open-mouthed at the brilliant illumination of a hall? They never do so at the millionfold brighter sunshine of noonday.

And so, in music, the signs have assumed greater consequence than that which they ought to stand for, and can only suggest.

How important, indeed, are "Third," "Fifth," and "Octave"! How strictly we divide "consonances" from "dissonances" – *in a sphere where no dissonances can possibly exist*!

We have divided the octave into twelve equidistant degrees, because we had to manage somehow, and have constructed our instruments in such a way that we can never get in above or below or between them. Keyboard instruments, in particular, have so thoroughly schooled our ears that we are no longer capable of hearing anything else – incapable of hearing except through this impure medium. Yet Nature created an *infinite gradation – infinite!* who still knows it nowadays?[13]

And within this duodecimal octave we have marked out a series of fixed intervals, seven in number, and founded thereon our entire art of music. What do I say – *one* series? Two such series, one for each leg: The Major and Minor Scales. When we start this series of intervals on some other degree of our semitonic ladder, we obtain a *new key*, and a "foreign" one, at that! How violently contracted a system arose from this initial confusion,[14] may be read in the law-books; we will not repeat it here.

We teach four-and-twenty keys, twelve times the two Series of Seven; but, in point of fact, we have at our command only two, the major key and the minor key. *The rest are merely transpositions.* By means of the several transpositions we are supposed to get different shades of harmony; but this is an illusion. In England, under the reign of the high "concert pitch," the most familiar works may be played a semitone higher than they are written, without changing their effect. Singers transpose an aria to suit their convenience, leaving untransposed what precedes and follows. Song-writers not infrequently publish their own compositions in three different pitches; in all three editions the pieces are precisely alike.

When a well-known face looks out of a window, it matters not whether it gazes down from the first story or the third.

Were it feasible to elevate or depress a landscape, far as eye can reach, by several hundred yards, the pictorial impression would neither gain nor lose by it.

Upon the two Series of Seven, the major key and the minor key, the whole art of music has been established; one limitation brings on the other.

To each of these a definite character has been attributed; we have learned and have taught that they should be heard as contrasts, and they have gradually acquired the significance of symbols: – Major and Minor – Maggiore e Minore – Contentment and Discontent – Joy and Sorrow – Light and Shade. The harmonic symbols have fenced in the expression of music, from Bach to Wagner, and yet further on until to-day and the day after to-morrow. *Minor* is employed with the same intention, and has the same effect upon us now, as two hundred years ago. Nowadays it is no longer possible to "compose" a funeral march, for it already exists, once for all. Even the least informed non-professional knows what to expect when a funeral march – whichever you please – is to be played. Even such an one can anticipate the difference between a symphony in major and one in minor. We are tyrannized by Major and Minor – by the bifurcated garment.

Strange, that one should feel major and minor as opposites. They both present the same face, now more joyous, now more serious; and a mere touch of the brush suffices to turn the one into the other. The passage from either to the other is easy and imperceptible; when it occurs frequently and swiftly, the two begin to shimmer and coalesce indistinguishably. – But when we recognize that major and minor form one Whole with a double meaning, and that the "four-and-twenty keys" are simply an elevenfold transposition of the original twain, we arrive unconstrainedly at a perception of the UNITY *of our system of keys* [tonality]. The conceptions of "related" and "foreign" keys vanish, and with them the entire intricate theory of degrees and relations. *We possess one single key.* But it is of most meagre sort.

"Unity of the key-system."

—"I suppose you mean that 'key' and 'key-system' are the sunbeam and its diffraction into colors?"

No; that I can not mean. For our whole system of tone, key, and tonality, taken in its entirety, is only a part of a fraction of one diffracted ray from that Sun, "Music," in the empyrean of the "eternal harmony."

However deeply rooted the attachment to the habitual, and inertia, may be in the ways and nature of humankind, in equal measure are energy, and opposition to the existing order, characteristic of all that has life. Nature has her wiles, and persuades man, obstinately opposed though he be to progress and change; Nature progresses continually and changes unremittingly, but with so even and unnoticeable movement that men perceive only quiescence. Only on looking backward from a distance do they note with astonishment that they have been deceived.

The Reformer of any given period excites irritation for the reason that his changes find men unprepared, and, above all, because these changes are appreciable. The Reformer, in comparison with Nature, is undiplomatic; and, as a wholly logical consequence, his changes do not win general acceptance until Time, with subtle, imperceptible advance, has bridged over the leap of the self-assured leader. Yet we find cases in which the reformer marched abreast of the times, while the rest fell behind. And then they have to be forced and lashed to take the leap across the passage they have missed. I believe that the major-and-minor key with its transpositional relations, our "twelve-semitone system," exhibits such a case of falling behind.

That some few have already felt how the intervals of the Series of Seven might be differently arranged (graduated) is manifested in isolated passages by Liszt, and recently by Debussy and his following, and even by Richard Strauss. Strong impulse, longing, gifted instinct, all speak from these strains. Yet it does not appear to me that a conscious and orderly conception of this intensified means of expression had been formed by these composers.

I have made an attempt to exhaust the possibilities of the arrangement of degrees within the seven-tone scale; and succeeded, by raising and lowering the intervals, in establishing *one hundred and thirteen different scales*. These 113 scales (within the octave *C-C*) comprise the greater part of our familiar twenty-four keys, and, furthermore, a series of new keys of peculiar character. But with these the mine is not exhausted, for we are at liberty to *transpose* each one of these 113, besides the blending of two such keys in harmony and melody.

There is a significant difference between the sound of the scale *c-db-eb-fb-gb-ab-bb-c* when *c* is taken as tonic, and the scale of *db* minor. By giving it the customary *C*-major triad as a fundamental harmony, a novel harmonic sensation is obtained. But now listen to this same scale supported alternately by the *A*-minor, *Eb*-major, and *C*-major triads, and you cannot avoid a feeling of delightful surprise at the strangely unfamiliar euphony.

But how would a lawgiver classify the tone-series *c-db-eb-fb-g-a-b-c*, *c-db-eb-f-gb-a-b-c*, *c-d-eb-fb-gb-a-b-c*, *c-db-e-f-gb-a-bb-c*? – or these, forsooth: *c-d-eb-fb-g-a#-b-c*, *c-d-eb-fb-g#-a-b-c*, *c-db-eb-f#-g#-a-bb-c*?

One cannot estimate at a glance what wealth of melodic and harmonic expression would thus be opened up to the hearing; but a great many novel possibilities may be accepted as certain, and are perceptible at a glance.

With this presentation, the unity of all keys may be considered as finally pronounced and justified. A kaleidoscopic blending and interchanging of twelve semitones within the three-mirror tube of Taste, Emotion, and Intention – the essential feature of the harmony of to-day.

The harmony of *to-day*, and not for long; for all signs presage a revolution, and a next step toward that "eternal harmony." Let us once again call to mind, that in this latter the gradation of the octave is *infinite*, and let us strive to draw a little nearer to infinitude. The tripartite tone (third of a tone) has for some time been demanding admittance, and we have left the call unheeded. Whoever has experimented, like myself (in a modest way), with this interval, and introduced (either with voice or with violin) two equidistant intermediate tones between the extremes of a whole tone, schooling his ear and his precision of attack, will not have failed to discern that tripartite tones are wholly independent intervals with a pronounced character, and not to be confounded with ill-tuned semitones. They form a refinement in chromatics based, as at present appears, on the whole-tone scale. Were we to adopt them without further preparation, we should have to give up the semitones and lose our "minor third" and "perfect fifth;" and this loss would be felt more keenly than the relative gain of a system of eighteen one-third tones.

But there is no apparent reason for giving up the semitones for the sake of this new system. By retaining, for each whole tone, a semitone, we obtain a second series of whole tones lying a semitone higher than the original series. Then, by dividing this second series of whole tones into third-tones, each third-tone in the lower series will be matched by a semitone in the higher series.

Thus we have really arrived at a system of whole tones divided into sixths of a tone; and we may be sure that even sixth-tones will sometime be adopted into musical speech. But the tonal system above sketched must first of all train the hearing to thirds of a tone, without giving up the semitones.

To summarize: We may set up either two series of third-tones, with an interval of a semitone between the series; or, the usual semitonic series *thrice repeated* at the interval of one-third of a tone.

Merely for the sake of distinction, let us call the first tone *C*, and the next third-tones *C#*, and *Db*; the first semitone (small) *c*, and its following thirds *c#* and *db*; the result is fully explained by the table below:

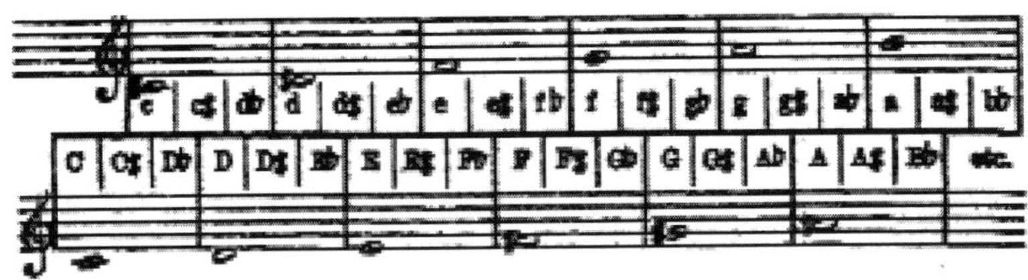

A preliminary expedient for notation might be, to draw six lines for the staff, using the lines for the whole tones and the spaces for the semitones:

then indicating the third-tones by sharps and flats:

The question of notation seems to me subordinate. On the other hand, the question is important and imperious, how and on what these tones are to be produced. Fortunately, while busied with this essay, I received from America direct and authentic intelligence which solves the problem in a simple manner. I refer to an invention by Dr. Thaddeus Cahill.[15] He has constructed a comprehensive apparatus which makes it possible to transform an electric current into a fixed and mathematically exact number of vibrations. As pitch depends on the number of vibrations, and the apparatus may be "set" on any number desired, the infinite gradation of the octave may be accomplished by merely moving a lever corresponding to the pointer of a quadrant.

Only a long and careful series of experiments, and a continued training of the ear, can render this unfamiliar material approachable and plastic for the coming generation, and for Art.

And what a vista of fair hopes and dreamlike fancies is thus opened for them both! Who has not dreamt that he could float on air? and firmly believed his dream to be reality? – Let us take thought, how music may be restored to its primitive, natural essence; let us free it from architectonic, acoustic and esthetic dogmas; let it be pure invention and sentiment, in harmonies, in forms, in tone-colors (for invention and sentiment are not the prerogative of melody alone); let it follow the line of the rainbow and vie with the clouds in breaking sunbeams; *let Music be naught else than Nature mirrored by and reflected from the human breast*; for it is sounding air and floats above and beyond the air; within Man himself as universally and absolutely as in Creation entire; for it can gather together and disperse without losing in intensity.

In his book "Beyond Good and Evil" (*Jenseits von Gut und Böse*) Nietzsche says: "With regard to German music I consider precaution necessary in various ways. Assuming that a person loves the South (as I love it) as a great training-school for health of soul and sense in their highest potency, as an uncontrollable flood and glamour of sunshine spreading over a race of independent and self-reliant beings; – well, such an one will learn to be more or less on his guard against German music, because, while spoiling his taste anew, it undermines his health. "Such a Southlander (not by descent, but by belief) must, should he dream of the future of music, likewise dream of a redemption of music from the North, while in his ears there rings the prelude to a deeper, mightier, perchance a more evil and more mysterious music, a super-German music, which does not fade, wither and die away in view of the blue, sensuous sea and the splendor of Mediterranean skies, as all German music does; – a super-European music, that asserts itself even amid the tawny sunsets of the desert, whose soul is allied with the palm-tree, and can consort and prowl with great, beautiful, lonely beasts of prey.

"I could imagine a music whose rarest charm should consist in its complete divorce from the Good and the Bad; – only that its surface might be ruffled, as it were, by a longing as of a sailor for home, by variable golden shadows and tender frailties: – an Art which should see fleeing toward it, from afar off, the hues of a perishing moral world become wellnigh incomprehensible, and which should be hospitable and profound enough to harbor such belated fugitives."

And Tolstoi transmutes a landscape-impression into a musical impression when he writes, in "Lucerne": "Neither on the lake, nor on the mountains, nor in the skies, a single straight line, a single unmixed color, a single point of repose; – everywhere movement, irregularity, caprice, variety, an incessant interplay of shades and lines, and in it all the reposefulness, softness, harmony and inevitableness of Beauty."

Will this music ever be attained?

"Not all reach Nirvana; but he who, gifted from the beginning, learns everything that one ought to learn, experiences all that one should experience, renounces what one should renounce, develops what one should develop, realizes what one should realize – he shall reach Nirvana."[16] (Kern, *Geschichte des Buddhismus in Indien.*)

If Nirvana be the realm "beyond the Good and the Bad," *one* way leading thither is here pointed out. A way to the very portal. To the bars that divide Man from Eternity – or that open to admit that which was temporal. Beyond that portal sounds *music*. Not the strains of "musical art.[17] – It may be, that we must leave Earth to find that music. But only to the pilgrim who has succeeded on the way in freeing himself from earthly shackles, shall the bars open.

ADDENDA

Feeling – like honesty – is a moral point of honor, an attribute of whose possession no one will permit denial, which claims a place in life and art alike. But while, in life, a want of feeling may be forgiven to the possessor of a more brilliant attribute, such as bravery or impartial justice, in art feeling is held to be the highest moral qualification.

In music, however, feeling requires two consorts, taste and style. Now, in life, one encounters real taste as seldom as deep and true feeling; as for style, it is a province of art. What remains, is a species of pseudo-emotion which must be characterized as lachrymose hysteria or turgidity. And, above all, people insist upon having it plainly paraded before their eyes! It must be underscored, so that everybody shall stop, look, and listen. The audience sees it, greatly magnified, thrown on the screen, so that it dances before the vision in vague, importunate vastness; it is cried on the streets, to summon them that dwell remote from art; it is gilded, to make the destitute stare in amaze.

For in life, too, the *expressions* of feeling, by mien and words, are oftenest employed; rarer, and more genuine, is that feeling which acts without talk; and most precious is the feeling which hides itself.

"Feeling" is generally understood to mean tenderness, pathos, and extravagance, of expression. But how much more does the marvelous flower "Emotion" enfold! Restraint and forbearance, renunciation, power, activity, patience, magnanimity, joyousness, and that all-controlling intelligence wherein feeling actually takes its rise.

It is not otherwise in Art, which holds the mirror up to Life; and still more outspokenly in Music, which repeats the emotions of Life – though for this, as I have said, taste and style must be added; Style, which distinguishes Art from Life.

What the amateur and the mediocre artist attempt to express, is feeling in little, in detail, for a short stretch.

Feeling on a grand scale is mistaken by the amateur, the semi-artist, the public (and the critics too, unhappily!), for a want of emotion, because they all are unable to hear the longer reaches as parts of a yet more extended whole. Feeling, therefore, is likewise economy.

Hence, I distinguish feeling as Taste, as Style, as Economy. Each a whole in itself, and each one-third of the Whole. Within and over them rules a subjective trinity: Temperament, Intelligence, and the instinct of Equipoise.

These six carry on a dance of such subtility in the choice of partners and intertwining of figures, in the bearing and the being borne, in advancing and curtesying, in motion and repose, that no loftier height of artistry is conceivable.

When the chords of the two triads are in perfect tune, Fantasy may – nay, must – associate with Feeling; supported by the Six, she will not degenerate, and out of this combination of all the elements arises Individuality. The individuality catches, like a lens, the light-impressions, reflects them, according to its nature, as a negative, and the hearer perceives the true picture.

In so far as taste participates in feeling, the latter – like all else – alters its forms of expression with the period. That is, one aspect or another of feeling will be favored at one time or another, onesidedly cultivated, especially developed. Thus, with and after Wagner, voluptuous sensuality came to the fore; the form of *intensification of passion* is still unsurmounted by contemporary composers. On every tranquil beginning followed a swift upward surge. Wagner, in this point insatiable, but not inexhaustible, turned from sheer necessity to the expedient, after reaching a climax, of starting afresh softly, to soar to a sudden new intensification.

Modern French writers exhibit a revulsion; their feeling is a reflexive chastity, or perhaps rather a restrained sensualism; the upstriving mountain-paths of Wagner are succeeded by monotonous plains of twilight uniformity.

Thus "style" forms itself out of feeling, when led by taste.

The "Apostles of the Ninth Symphony" have devised the notion of "depth" in music. It is still current at face-value, especially in Germanic lands.

There is a depth of feeling, and a depth of thought; the latter is literary, and can have no application to tones. Depth of feeling, by contrast, is psychical, and thoroughly germane to the nature of music. The Apostles of the Ninth Symphony have a peculiar and not quite clearly defined estimate of "depth" in music. *Depth* becomes *breadth*, and the attempt is made to attain it through *weight*; it then discovers itself (through an association of ideas) by a preference for a *deep register*, and (as I have had opportunity to observe) by the insinuation of a second, mysterious notion, usually of a literary sort. If these are not the sole specific signs, they are the most important ones.

To every disciple of philosophy, however, depth of feeling would seem to imply exhaustiveness in feeling, a complete absorption in the given mood.

Whoever, surrounded by the full tide of a genuine carnival crowd, slinks about morosely or even indifferently, neither affected nor carried away by the tremendous self-satire of mask and motley, by the might of misrule over law, by the vengeful feeling of wit running riot, shows himself incapable of sounding the depths of feeling. This gives further confirmation of the fact, that depth of feeling roots in a complete absorption in the given mood, however frivolous, and blossoms in the interpretation of that mood; whereas the current conception of deep feeling singles out only one aspect of feeling in man, and specializes that.

In the so-called "Champagne Aria" in Don Giovanni there lies more "depth" than in many a funeral march or nocturne: – Depth of feeling also shows in not wasting it on subordinate or unimportant matters.

Routine is highly esteemed and frequently required; in musical "officialdom" it is a *sine qua non*. That routine in music should exist at all, and, furthermore, that it can be nominated as a condition in the musician's bond, is another proof of the narrow confines of our musical art. Routine signifies the acquisition of a modicum of experience and artcraft, and their application to all cases which may occur; hence, there must be an astounding number of analogous cases. Now, I like to imagine a species of art-praxis wherein each case should be a new one, an exception! How helpless and impotent would the army of practical musicians stand before it! – in the end they would surely beat a retreat, and disappear. Routine transforms the temple of art into a factory. It destroys creativeness. For creation means, the bringing form out of the void; whereas routine flourishes on imitation. It is "poetry made to order." It rules because it suits the generality: In the theatre, in the orchestra, in virtuosi, in instruction. One longs to exclaim, "Avoid routine! Let each beginning be, as had none been before! Know nothing, but rather think and feel! For, behold, the myriad strains that once shall sound have existed since the beginning, ready, afloat in the æther, and together with them other myriads that shall never be heard. Only stretch forth your hands, and ye shall grasp a blossom, a breath of the sea-breeze, a sunbeam; avoid routine, for it strives to grasp only that wherewith your four walls are filled, and the same over and over again; the spirit of ease so infects you, that you will scarcely leave your armchairs, and will lay hold only of what is nearest to hand. And myriad strains are there since the beginning, still waiting for manifestation!"

"It is my misfortune, to possess no routine," Wagner once wrote Liszt, when the composition of "Tristan" was making no progress. Thus Wagner deceived himself, and wore a mask for others. He had too much routine, and his composing-machinery was thrown out of gear, just when a tangle formed in the mesh which only inspiration could unloose. True, Wagner found the clew when he succeeded in throwing off routine; but had he really never possessed it, he would have declared the fact without bitterness. And, after all, this sentence in Wagner's letter expresses the true artist-contempt for routine, inasmuch as he waives all claim to a qualification which he thinks meanly of, and takes care that others may not invest him with it. This self-praise he utters with a mien of ironic desperation. He is, in very truth, unhappy that composition is at a standstill, but finds rich consolation in the consciousness that his genius is above the cheap expedients of routine; at the same time, with an air of modesty, he sorrowfully confesses that he has not acquired a training belonging to the craft.

The sentence is a masterpiece of the native cunning of the instinct of self-preservation; but equally proves – and that is our point – the pettiness of routine in creative work.

Rspect the Pianoforte! Its disadvantages are evident, decided, and unquestionable: The lack of sustained tone, and the pitiless, unyielding adjustment of the inalterable semitonic scale. But its advantages and prerogatives approach the marvelous.

It gives a single man command over something complete; in its potentialities from softest to loudest in one and the same register it excels all other instruments. The trumpet can blare, but not sigh; contrariwise the flute; the pianoforte can do both. Its range embraces the highest and deepest practicable tones. Respect the Pianoforte!

Let doubters consider how the pianoforte was esteemed by Bach, Mozart, Beethoven, Liszt, who dedicated their choicest thoughts to it.

And the pianoforte has one possession wholly peculiar to itself, an inimitable device, a photograph of the sky, a ray of moonlight – the Pedal.

The effects of the pedal are unexhausted, because they have remained even to this day the drudges of a narrow-souled and senseless harmonic theory; the treatment accorded them is like trying to mould air or water into geometric forms. Beethoven, who incontestably achieved the greatest progress on and for the pianoforte, divined the mysteries of the pedal, and to him we owe the first liberties.

The pedal is in ill-repute. For this, absurd irregularities must bear the blame. Let us experiment with *sensible* irregularities.

"I felt ... that the book I shall write will be neither in English nor in Latin; and this for the one reason... namely, that the language in which it may be given me not only to write, but also to think, will not be Latin, or English, or Italian, or Spanish, but a language not even one of whose words I know, a language in which dumb things speak to me, and in which, it may be, I shall at last have to respond in my grave to an Unknown Judge."

(Von Hofmannsthal: A letter.)

NOTES

1. None the less, in these arts, taste and individuality can and will unceasingly find refreshment and rejuvenation.
2. Tradition is a plaster mask taken from life, which, in the course of many years, and after passing through the hands of innumerable artisans, leaves its resemblance to the original largely a matter of imagination.
3. In the recitatives of his Passions we hear "human speech"; *not* "correct declamation."
4. As characteristic traits of Beethoven's individuality I would mention the poetic fire, the strong human feeling (whence springs his revolutionary temper), and a portent of modern nervousness. These traits are certainly opposed to those of a "classic." Moreover, Beethoven is no "master," as the term applies to Mozart or the later Wagner, just because his art foreshadows a greater, as yet incomplete. (Compare the section next-following.)
5. "Together with the problem, it gives us the solution," as I once said of Mozart.
6. "...Beethoven, dont les esquisses *thématiques ou élémentaires* sont innombrables, mais qui, sitôt les thèmes trouvés, semble par cela même en avoir établi tout le développement..." [Vincent d'Indy, in "César Franck."]
7. How strongly notation influences style in music, and fetters

imagination, how "form" grew up out of it and from form arose "conventionalism" in expression, is shown very convincingly and avenges itself in tragic wise in E. T. A. Hoffmann, who occurs to me here as a typical example. This remarkable man's mental conceptions, lost in visionary moods and revelling in transcendentalism, as his writings set forth in oft inimitable fashion, must naturally – so one would infer – have found in the dreamlike and transcendental art of tones a language and mode of expression peculiarly congenial. The veil of mysticism, the secret harmonies of Nature, the thrill of the supernatural, the twilight vagueness of the borderland of dreams, everything, in fact, which he so effectively limned with the precision of *words* – all this, one would suppose, he could have interpreted to fullest effect by the aid of music. And yet, comparing Hoffmann's best musical work with the weakest of his literary productions, you will discover to your sorrow how a conventional system of measures, periods and keys – whereto the hackneyed opera-style of the time adds its share – could turn a poet into a Philistine. But that his fancy cherished another ideal of music, we learn from many, and frequently admirable, observations of Hoffmann the *littérateur*.

8. The only kind of people one might properly call *musical*, are the singers; for they themselves can sound. Similarly, a clown who by some trick produces tones when he is touched, might be called a *pseudo-musical* person.

9. "But these pieces are so musical," a violinist once remarked to me of a four-hand worklet which I had characterized as trivial.

10. "My dog is *very* musical," I have heard said in all seriousness. Should the dog take precedence of Berlioz?

11. Such has been my own fate.

12. With a friend I once indulged in such trifling in order to ascertain how many commonly known compositions were written according to the scheme of the second theme in the Adagio of the Ninth Symphony. In a few moments we had collected some fifteen analogues of the most different kinds, among them specimens of the lowest type of art. And Beethoven himself: – Is the theme of the Finale in the "Fifth" any other than the one wherewith the "Second" introduces its

Allegro? – or than the principal theme of the Third Piano Concerto, only in minor?

13. "The equal temperament of 12 degrees, which was discussed theoretically as early as about 1500, but not established as a principle until shortly before 1700 (by Andreas Werkmeister), divides the octave into twelve equal portions (semitones, hence 'twelve-semitone system') through which mean values are obtained; no interval is perfectly pure, but all are fairly serviceable." (Riemann, "Musik-Lexikon.") Thus, through Andreas Werkmeister, this master-workman in art, we have gained the "twelve-semitone" system with intervals which are all impure, but fairly serviceable. But what is "pure," and what "impure"? We hear a piano "gone out of tune," and whose intervals may thus have become "pure, but unserviceable," and it sounds *impure* to us. The diplomatic "Twelve-semitone system" is an invention mothered by necessity; yet none the less do we sedulously guard its imperfections.

14. It is termed "The Science of Harmony."

15. "New Music for an Old World." Dr. Thaddeus Cahill's Dynamophone, an extraordinary electrical invention for producing scientifically perfect music. Article in McClure's Magazine for July, 1906, by Ray Stannard Baker. Readers interested in the details of this invention are referred to the above-mentioned magazine article.

16. As if anticipating my thoughts, M. Vincent d'Indy has just written me: "... laissant de côté les contingences et les petitesses de la vie pour regarder constamment vers un idéal qu'on ne pourra jamais atteindre, mais dont il est permis de se rapprocher."

17. I think I have read, somewhere, that Liszt confined his Dante Symphony to the two movements, *Inferno* and *Purgatorio*, "because our tone-speech is inadequate to express the felicities of Paradise."

CHROMATIC MUSIC

BRUNO CORRA

1912

It could be said that the only display of the art of colors currently in use is the painting. A painting is a medley of colors placed in reciprocal relationships in order to represent an idea. (You will note that I have defined painting as the art of color. For brevity's sake, I will not concern myself with line, an element taken from another art.) A new and more rudimentary form of pictorial art can be created by placing masses of color harmoniously arranged in relationship to each other over a surface, so as to give pleasure to the eye without representing any image. This would correspond to what in music is known as harmony, and we can therefore call it chromatic harmony. These two forms of art, chromatic harmony and the painting, are spatial; music tells us of the existence of something essentially different, the mingling of chromatic tones presented to the eye successively, a motif of colors, a chromatic theme. I shall not, since it is not yet necessary, go on to speak of a fourth form of art, corresponding to musical drama, which would give rise to chromatic drama.

Consequently, two years ago, after the entire theory had been minutely established, we decided to make a serious attempt to create a music of colors. We immediately began to think of the instruments, which perhaps did not exist, and which we would have to have made to order, to enable us to realize these theories. We traveled untrodden roads, letting intuition guide us for the most part, but always proceeding concurrently, in order not to be led astray, with our study of the physics of light and sound, the works of Tyndall and of many others.

Naturally we applied and exploited the laws of parallelism between the arts which had already been determined. For two months each studied on his own without communicating his results – afterwards we presented, discussed and amalgamated our observations. This confirmed our idea, which had anyway preceded our study of physics, of adhering to music and transferring the tempered scale of music into the field of color. We knew, however, that the chromatic scale consists of only one octave, and that, on the other hand, the eye, unlike the ear, does not possess the power of resolution (although, rethinking this point, I realize that one must have reservations). Yet we felt the obvious need of a subdivision of the solar spectrum, even an artificial and arbitrary one (since the effect stems principally from the relationships between the colors that impress the eye). Consequently we selected four equally distanced gradations in each color. We had four reds chosen at equal distances in the spectrum, four greens, four violets, etc. In this way we managed to extend the seven colors in four octaves. After the violet of the first octave came the red of the second, and so on. To translate all this into practice we naturally used a series of twenty-eight colored electric light bulbs, corresponding to twenty-eight keys. Each bulb was fitted with an oblong reflector: the first experiments were done with direct light, and in the subsequent ones a sheet of ground glass was placed in front of the light bulb. The keyboard was exactly like that of a piano (but was less extensive). When an octave was played, for example, the two colors were mingled, as are two sounds on the piano.

This chromatic piano, when it was tried out, gave quite good results, so much so that at first we were under the illusion that we had resolved the problem definitively. We amused ourselves by finding all sorts of chromatic mixtures, we composed a few color sonatinas – notturni in violet and mattinate in green. We translated, with a few necessary modifications, a Venetian barcarolle by Mendelssohn, a rondo by Chopin, a Mozart sonata. But at last, after three months of experimentation, we had to confess that with these means no further progress could be made. We obtained the most graceful effects, it is true, but never to the extent that we felt fully gripped. We had at our disposition only twenty-eight tones, the fusions did not work well, the sources of light were not strong enough, if we used powerful bulbs the excessive heat made them discolor in a few days, and then we had to recolor them exactly, with considerable loss of time. We felt very clearly that, in order to obtain the large orchestral effects which alone can convince the masses, we needed to have a truly stupefying intensity of light at our disposition – only then could we emerge from the restricted field of scientific experiment to enter directly into its practice

THE PAINTING OF SOUNDS, NOISES AND SMELLS

CARLO CARRÀ

11 August 1913

Before the 19th century, painting was the art of silence. Painters of antiquity, of the Renaissance, of the 17th and 18th centuries, never envisaged the possibility of rendering sounds, noises and smells in painting, even when they chose flowers, stormy seas or wild skies as their subjects.

In their bold revolution, the Impressionists made some confused, hesitant attempts at sounds and noises in their pictures. Before them nothing, absolutely nothing!

However, we should point out at once that between the Impressionists' swarming brush-strokes and our Futurist paintings of sounds, noises and smells there is an enormous difference, like the contrast between a misty winter morning and a sweltering summer afternoon, or to put it better, between the first signs of pregnancy and an adult man in his fully developed strength.

In the Impressionist canvases, sounds and noises are expressed in such a thin, faded way that they might have been perceived by the eardrum of a deaf man. This is not the place for a detailed account of the principles and experiments of the Impressionists. There is no need to enquire minutely into all the reasons why the Impressionists never succeeded in painting sounds, noises and smells. We shall only mention here what they would have had to drop to obtain results:

1. The extremely vulgar trompe-l'oeil, a game worthy of an academic of the Leonardo da Vinci sort or a foolish set-designer of realistic operas.

2. The concept of color harmonies, a characteristic concept and defect of the French which inevitably forces them into Watteau-style prettiness and an abuse of light blues, pale greens, mauves and pinks. We have said more than once how much we despise this tendency towards soft, feminine, gentle effects.

3. Contemplative idealism, which I have defined as a sentimental mimicry of natural appearances. This contemplative idealism contaminates the pictorial construction of the Impressionists, just as it contaminated those of their predecessors, Corot and Delacroix.

4. Anecdote and detail, which (although it it a reaction and an antidote to false academical construction) almost always leads them to photographical reproduction. As for the Post- and Neo-Impressionists, such as Matisse, Signac and Seurat, we see that far from perceiving the problem and dealing with the difficulties of sounds, noises and smells in their paintings, they preferred to withdraw into static representations in order to obtain a greater synthesis of form (Matisse) and a systematic application of light (Signac, Seurat).

We Futurists therefore claim that in bringing the elements of sound, noise and smell to painting we are opening fresh paths. We have already taught artists to love our essentially dynamic modern life with its sounds, noises and smells, thereby destroying the stupid passion for values which are solemn, academic, serene, hieratic and mummified: everything purely intellectual, in fact. Imagination without strings, words-in-freedom, the systematic use of onomatopoeia, antigraceful music without rhythmic quadrature, and the art of noises — these were created by the same Futurist sensibility that has given birth to the painting of sounds, noises and smells.

It is indisputably true that (1) silence is static and sounds, noises and smells are dynamic; (2) sounds, noises and smells are nothing but different forms and intensities of vibration; and (3) any succession of sounds, noises and smells impresses on the mind an arabesque of form and color. We must measure this intensity and perceive these arabesques.

The painting of sounds, noises and smells rejects:

1. All muted colors, even those obtained directly and without using tricks like patinas and glazes.

2. The banality of those velvets, silks and flesh tints which are too human, too refined, too soft, and flowers which are too pale and drooping.

3. Greys, browns and all muddy colors.

4. The use of pure horizontal and vertical lines, and all other dead lines.

5. The right angle, which we consider passionless.

6. The cube, the pyramid and all other static shapes.

7. The unities of time and place.

The painting of sounds, noises and smells calls for:

1. Reds, rrrrreds, the rrrrrreddest rrrrrrreds that shouuuuuuut.

2. Greens, that can never be greener, greeeeeeeeeeeens that screeeeeeam, yellows, as violent as can be: polenta yellows, saffron yellows, brass yellows.

3. All the colors of speed, of joy, of carousings and fantastic carnivals, of fireworks, cafe-chantants and music-halls; all colors seen in movement, colors experienced in time and not in space.

4. The dynamic arabesque, which is the sole reality created by the artist in the depths of his feeling.

5. The clash of all the acute angles, which we have already called the angles of will.

6. Oblique lines which fall on the observer like so many bolts from the blue, along with lines of depth.

7. The sphere, the ellipse that spins, the upside-down cone, the spiral and all the dynamic forms which the infinite powers of an artist's genius are able to uncover.

8. Perspective obtained not as the objectivity of distances but as a subjective interpenetration of hard and soft, sharp and dull forms.

9. As a universal subject and as the sole reason for a painting's existence: the significance of its dynamic construction (polyphonic architectural whole). Architecture is usually thought of as something static; this is wrong. What we have in mind is an architecture similar to the dynamic musical architecture achieved by the Futurist musician Pratella. Architecture is found in the movement of colors, of smoke from a chimney, and in metallic structures, when they are experienced in a violent, chaotic state of mind.

10. The inverted cone (the natural shape of an explosion), the slanting cylinder and cone.

11. The collision of two cones at their apexes (the natural shape of a water spout) with flexible or curving lines (a clown jumping, dancers).

12. The zig-zag and the wavy line.

13. Ellipsoidal curves considered as straight lines in movement.

14. Lines and volumes seen as plastic transcendentalism, that is, according to their characteristic degree of curvature or obliqueness, determined by the painter's state of mind.

15. Echoes of lines and volumes in movement.

16. Plastic complementarism (for both forms and colors),

based on the law of equivalent contrasts and on the opposite poles of the spectrum. This complementarism derives from an imbalance of forms (which are hence forced to move) The consequent elimination of the complements of volumes. We must reject these because like a pair of crutches they allow only a single movement, forward and backward, and not the total movement that we call spherical expansion in space.

17. The continuity and simultaneity of the plastic transcendency of the animal mineral, vegetable and mechanical kingdoms.

18. Abstract plastic wholes, corresponding not to our sight but to the sensations which derive from sounds, noises, smells and all the unknown forces that surround us.

These polyphonic and polyrhythmic abstract plastic wholes correspond to a requirement of inner enharmonics that we Futurist painters believe to be indispensable to pictorial sensibility.

These plastic wholes have a mysterious fascination and are more meaningful than those created by our visual and tactile senses, being closer to our pure plastic spirit.

We Futurist painters maintain that sounds noises and smells are incorporated in the expression of lines, volumes and colors just as lines, volumes and colors are incorporated in the architecture of a musical work. Our canvases will therefore express the plastic equivalents of the sounds noises and smells found in theaters, music-halls, cinemas, brothels, railway stations, ports, garages, hospitals, workshops, etc., etc.

From the point of view of form: sounds, noises and smells can be concave, convex triangular, ellipsoidal, oblong, conical, spherical, spiral, etc.

From the point of view of colour: sounds, noises and smells can be yellow, green, dark blue, light blue or purple. In railway stations and garages, and throughout the mechanical and sporting world, sounds, noises and smells are predominantly red; in restaurants and cafes they are silver, yellow and purple. While the sounds, noises and smells of animals are yellow and blue, those of a woman are green, blue and purple.

We do not exaggerate in claiming that smell alone is enough to create in our minds arabesques of form and color which can constitute the motive and justify the necessity of a painting. In fact, if we are shut in a dark room (so that our sense of sight no longer functions) with flowers petrol or other strong-smelling things, our plastic spirit gradually eliminates the memory sensations and constructs particular plastic wholes whose quality of weight and movement corresponds perfectly to the smells found in the room. These smells, through an obscure process, have become an environment-force, determining that state of mind which for us Futurist painters constitutes a pure plastic whole.

This bubbling and whirling of forms and lights composed of sounds, noises and smells has been partly rendered by me in my *Anarchist's Funeral* and *Jolts Of A Taxi-cab*; by Boccioni in *States Of Mind* and *Forces Of A Street*; by Russolo in *Revolt*; and by Severini in *Pan Pan*, paintings which aroused violent controversy at our first Paris Exhibition in 1912. This kind of bubbling over requires a powerful emotion, even delirium, on the part of the artist, who in order to render a vortex must be a vortex of sensation himself, a pictorial force and not a cold logical intellect.

This is the truth! In order to achieve this total painting, which requires the active cooperation of all the senses, a painting which is a plastic state of mind of the universal, you must paint, as drunkards sing and vomit, sounds, noises and smells!

THE MANIFESTO OF FUTURISM

F.T. MARINETTI

20 February 1909

1. We want to sing the love of danger, the habit of energy and rashness.

2. The essential elements of our poetry will be courage, audacity and revolt.

3. Literature has up to now magnified pensive immobility, ecstasy and slumber. We want to exalt movements of aggression, feverish sleeplessness, the double march, the perilous leap, the slap and the blow with the fist.

4. We declare that the splendor of the world has been enriched by a new beauty: the beauty of speed. A racing automobile with its bonnet adorned with great tubes like serpents with explosive breath... a roaring motor car which seems to run on machine-gun fire, is more beautiful than the Victory of Samothrace.

5. We want to sing the man at the wheel, the ideal axis of which crosses the earth, itself hurled along its orbit.

6. The poet must spend himself with warmth, glamour and prodigality to increase the enthusiastic fervor of the primordial elements.

7. Beauty exists only in struggle. There is no masterpiece that has not an aggressive character. Poetry must be a violent assault on the forces of the unknown, to force them to bow before man.

8. We are on the extreme promontory of the centuries! What is the use of looking behind at the moment when we must open the mysterious shutters of the impossible? Time and Space died yesterday. We are already living in the absolute, since we have already created eternal, omnipresent speed.

9. We want to glorify war – the only cure for the world – militarism, patriotism, the destructive gesture of the anarchists, the beautiful ideas which kill, and contempt for woman.

10. We want to demolish museums and libraries, fight morality, feminism and all opportunist and utilitarian cowardice.

11. We will sing of the great crowds agitated by work, pleasure and revolt; the multi-colored and polyphonic surf of revolutions in modern capitals: the nocturnal vibration of the arsenals and the workshops beneath their violent electric moons: the gluttonous railway stations devouring smoking serpents; factories suspended from the clouds by the thread of their smoke; bridges with the leap of gymnasts flung across the diabolic cutlery of sunny rivers: adventurous steamers sniffing the horizon; great-breasted locomotives, puffing on the rails like enormous steel horses with long tubes for bridle, and the gliding flight of aeroplanes whose propeller sounds like the flapping of a flag and the applause of enthusiastic crowds.

A CHRONOLOGY OF FUTURIST MUSIC AND NOISE

1909

20 February: *Le Figaro*, Paris, publishes the first **Futurist Manifesto** by F. T. Marinetti.

December: First performance of Balilla Pratella's musical Futurist work, *La Sina d'Vargöun*, at the Teatro Communale, Bologna . Pratella officially joined the Futurist group in 1910.

1910

Publication of Arnaldo Gina and Bruno Corra's chromatic music manifesto **Arte**.

1911

11 January: Balilla Pratella's **Manifesto Of Futurist Musicians**.

11 March: Balilla Pratella's **Technical Manifesto Of Futurist Music**.

1912

11 August: Balilla Pratella's **Destruction Of Quadrature**.

Publication of **Abstract Cinema / Chromatic Music** by Bruno Corra, who will officially join the group in 1916.

December: Birth of the Russian Futurist movement. Russian Futurist composers of the 1920s would include Mikhail Gnesin, Alexander Goedicke, Geog Kirkor, Julian Krein, and Alexander Mosolov.

1913

21 February: *Musica Futurista Per Orchestra* by Pratella performed at the Teatro Costanzi, Rome.

11 March: Luigi Russolo's manifesto **The Art Of Noises** published in Milan as a pamphlet.

June: *Intonorumori* (Noise Machines) built by Russolo and Ugo Piatti demonstrated at the Teatro Storchi, Modena.

Russolo's manifesto **The Futurist Intonorumori** published in Milan.

11 August: Carlo Carrà's **The Painting of Sounds, Noises And Smells**.

1914

21 April: The first public performance of *Intonorumori* at the Teatro dal Verme in Milan. Russolo, assisted by Ugo Piatti, performs three pieces (*Awakening Of A City*, *The Meeting Of Automobiles And Aeroplanes* and *Dining On The Hotel Terrace*) and is met with violent reaction.

June: Russolo and Marinetti give twelve performances of the *Intonarumori* at the London Coliseum.

July: Marinetti and other Futurists enlist in the Lombard Volunteer Cyclist Battalion, in preparation for war. Marinetti later reported that thirteen of their number were killed, and forty-one wounded.

1915

Private première of Balilla Pratella's opera *Aviatore Dro* (1914), written in close collaboration with Marinetti.

Fortunato Depero creates *Rumorgraphia* (Noise Graphism), a paper and ink study designed to represent the direction and volume of sound. He refers to this as *scrittura dei rumori* (writing in noise).

1916

March: Depero composes various “noise-songs”.

1917

Carrà leaves the Futurist movement; this signals the end of the first wave and the beginning of a second wave for the movement.

17 December: Russolo is seriously wounded in the head at Monte Grappa and requires cranial surgery; after 18 months of rehabilitation he recovers.

1919

Manifesto Of Synopsis Or Visual Transposition Of Music by Bragaglia, Luciani, and Casavola.

1921

1 March: **Manifesto Of Musical Improvisation** by Bartoccini and Mantia.

Russolo and his brother, Antonio, make a phonograph recording with works entitled *Corale* and *Serenata*, combining conventional orchestral music set against noise machines; this is thought to be their only surviving sound recording.

1922

Russolo develops the “Noise Harmonium” or *Rumorarmonio*.

1924

Franco Casavola’s **Futurist Music**.

Visual Synthesis Of Music by Casavola, Luciani, and Bragaglia.

Casavola's **Chromatic Atmospheres Of Music**.

Casavola's **Scenoplastic Versions Of Music**.

Casavola's **Illustrated Music**.

(Casavola's compositions include *Prelude To Prigionieri* and *Danza Della Scimmie*.)

1927

Release of Eugene Deslaw's film *La Marche Des Machines*, with original music by Russolo.

1931

Russolo develops the Enharmonic Piano.

1933

Futurist Manifesto Of The Musical City by the Futurist Group of Verona.

1934

Futurist Manifesto Of Geometric, Synthetic And Curative Aeromusic by Marinetti and Aldo Giuntini, who also composed *Sintesi Musicali Futuristiche*.

1944

Manifesto Of Musical Words: Alphabet In Freedom by Marinetti and Crali.

2 December: Marinetti dies of a heart attack in Bellagio, Como.